THIS IS ADVERTISING

The Ayer book on what advertising
is all about, who does what, and
how to get a job in it.

HARRY C. GROOME, JR.

1975

Published by AYER PRESS,West Washington Square, Philadelphia, Pa. 19106

AYER PRESS PUBLICATIONS

- Ayer Directory of Publications
  ($49.00 plus 82¢ postage and handling)
- Ayer Motel-Hotel Register
  ($18.95 plus 82¢ postage and handling)
- Ayer Glossary of Advertising and Related Terms
  ($8.90 plus 38¢ postage and handling)
- Ayer Fund-Raising Dinner Guide
  ($8.90 plus 38¢ postage and handling)
- Ayer Public Relations and Publicity Style Book
  ($9.95 plus 38¢ postage and handling)
- This Is Advertising (ad career guide)
  ($9.95 plus 38¢ postage and handling)

INTERNATIONAL
STANDARD BOOK NUMBER
0-910190-04-6

TABLE OF CONTENTS

INTRODUCTION

A distinguished practitioner of advertising, friend, and former associate recently described the advertising business this way:

"My oldest son once asked me to explain what I do for a living. I finally drew on a piece of paper a series of interlocking cog wheels in descending size from one foot in diameter through five stages to the final one an inch in diameter.

"The first cog wheel represented the master corporate goal of the client. The second cog represented the chief executive's policy. The third represented the marketing vice president's plan. The fourth represented the advertising director's instructions. The fifth represented my tasks.

"I told John that all I knew was that every time that big cog started turning an eighth of an inch, I spun 37½ times and had to work through the Christmas holidays."

The description is apt, and I am grateful to Tyler Macdonald for his permission to use it.

H.C.G.

I WHAT IS ADVERTISING

Any treatise worth its salt ought to start with a definition. Perhaps that's too obvious to require comment. Yet, in the case of advertising the curious thing is that there is no standard, universally accepted definition. Consequently, we'll have to commence by trying to supply one that will stand reasonably rigorous inspection.

Depending on the person you talk to, you'll hear advertising described as everything from the classic oversimplification of "salesmanship in print" to a devious device "by which people are compelled to buy things they neither want nor need." Like all cliches, these do not stand up in the face of serious investigation. The reason is relatively simple: advertising is used for such a variety of purposes and in such a broad spectrum of situations that it is entitled to a more thoughtful and useful definition.

Let us try to analyze it and see if we can come closer to something we can live with. To begin with, it is obviously a form of communication, a way of informing people about something someone wants them to know, understand, or act upon. Since there are many other ways to communicate, it is inevitable to insist that advertising is a form, or a method, or a technique for communicating. The preference here is for "method" as being slightly more precise than "form," and something less limiting than "technique." So let's settle for a "method of communication."

Next, communication with whom? People certainly. And equally certainly, large numbers of people: more people than can be managed practically through personal visits, telephone calls, letters or any other fairly intimate method you can think of. So that adds a dimension of size or mass to the definition, giving us a "method of mass communication."

Practicality was just mentioned as being important, and translated into commercial language that means affordability. Of all the known ways of communicating with great numbers of people advertising is the most affordable, the most efficient. As an example, an advertisement in a reasonably popular TV show or in a magazine like the *Reader's Digest* will be exposed to 1,000 viewers or readers at a cost of from $4.50 to $7.00. A thousand local phone calls would cost $100.00; the same number of post-cards, $80.00 for the postage alone without any charges for typing or handling. Moreover, personal letters would be correspondingly more. And personal conversations would entail staggering costs. So advertising is relatively economical and efficient.

What else? Control is most important to most advertisers in three ways: control over *what* is said, to *whom* it is said, and *when* it is said. To a very significant degree, advertising permits the element of control. It certainly allows the advertiser to word and illustrate his message in the way he wants, and to prescribe the time it appears. He can also control the audience for his message in a somewhat broader sense. A simple illustration of the point would be: if he had an outboard motor to sell he would be inclined to place an advertisement in *Motor Boating & Sailing*. Similarly, if he had an advanced formula for turkey feed he would probably use *Turkey World*. Thus, control is a key characteristic of advertising.

Further to illustrate this point, a publicity release—although it also can be a form of mass communication—is subject to the willingness of the publisher to use it at all, subject to the publisher's idea of when it should be used and,more importantly, how much of it should be used. Advertising encounters no such hazards.

Another characteristic of advertising is, or can be, speed. If there is something to be communicated to a lot of people quickly, advertising can accommodate that requirement satisfactorily. In a personal situation, a classified advertisement seeking the return of a lost dog can be arranged overnight. On the corporate scene, the same kind of thing can be accomplished when the occasion requires through the use of newspaper advertisements, radio spots and, with a little luck, even television spots.

Finally, every advertisement carries with it the element of responsibility of the advertiser who pays for it. With the exception of the "Box 2345" type classified advertisements, almost all advertisements identify the sponsoring individual or company. In this way, accountability and responsibility for what is said, implied, or promised, are clearly fixed.

Assuming that the foregoing is reasonable, logical and sensible, we should then have the following acceptable definition:

"Advertising is a method of mass communication characterized by economy, speed, control and responsibility."

This definition is sufficiently precise and, at the same time, sufficiently flexible to accommodate all the customary assignments that advertising is asked to carry out. The one we think of first, of course, is the job of persuading someone to buy something—a product or a service. This, of course, is the chief job of advertising. To keep things in perspective, however, it is a good idea to list some of the other tasks it is called on to do. They are things like these:

- Simply to inform, as in the case of changes in airline arrival and departure times, or of changes in business addresses.

- To list items for sale and their prices without trying to persuade anyone to buy any specific item. The big chain store newspaper advertisements are a prime example of this task.

- To identify a need, as in the case of most classified newspaper advertising whether it be lost and found, jobs wanted and jobs to be had, or any one of all the other uses that you can find in your local newspaper.

- To urge people to do something (not concerned with selling) like contributing to the United Fund or the Red Cross, or buying Christmas Seals.

- To change or strengthen opinions about issues as well as about companies or corporations. Often this assignment is that of offering simple information. An example would be explaining what a conglomerate corporation is and does and what its components are and do.

- To promote greater understanding of common problems that need to be met, as in the case of conservation of resources in times of shortages.

- To comply with various laws which require such things as the annual publication of bank earinings statements, or the probate of wills, and so on.

A significant observation to be made about a complete list of assignments for advertising is that it is very frequently used to urge people *not* to do something. A good case in point is all the commercials urging people not to smoke or not to use hard drugs. It is easy to recall quickly many other so-called negative appeals, which should help put advertising, and our definition of it, into proper perspective.

II ADVERTISING IN OUR SOCIETY

If we have reached agreement on what advertising is, we should next see how it fits into our modern social structure. No attempt will be made here to embark on a profound sociological safari. What can be done within the framework of this much simpler exposition, however, is to set forth some of the basic considerations useful in evaluating the fit of advertising to today's society. Is it a good thing or a bad thing? Or both good and bad? Or is it, as cold logic would lead us to conclude, neither good nor bad, except as each individual advertiser elects to use it?

Evaluation of these questions can be accomplished only if we understand the nature of our society: what it is and what it is not. This is a cardinal point. It is one that is often overlooked by both proponents and opponents of advertising.

The fact is that we live in an advanced industrial and technological age, and the United States is probably the prime example of that existence. Obviously, we are no longer an agrarian country—with its presumably simple virtues—nor one in an early developmental state. We have arrived where we are as the result of generations of competitive commercial activity supported by an enormous supply of natural resources. And even if we wanted to change that fact, we could not. Consequently, we should not allow ourselves the luxury of creating or assuming some other kind of civilization against which to evaluate the propriety of advertising, whatever it may be. As President Grover Cleveland once said: "We are faced with a condition..." And so we are, like it or not.

THIS IS ADVERTISING

The result of this condition—this competitive industrial society—is very simply that advertising is *a business necessity*. A fact that Ralph Waldo Emerson recognized in his famous remarks about the better mouse trap. The quotation begins this way: "I trust a good deal to common fame, as we all must." And it goes on from there. In business, "common fame" on a broad scale can come only as a result of advertising. A relatively uncomplicated case should serve to validate this conclusion. So let us examine for a moment a familiar repetitive business situation.

An entrepreneur hits on a new product idea or an improvement of an existing product. Usually with difficulty, he raises capital to produce and distribute his brainchild. Because of financial limitations, and also to minimize risk, he is likely to begin marketing on a local or regional basis. And one of the first things he *must* do to launch his product is to announce to the people in the area what it is, or does, and where it is available. Using conventional channels of communication, he now becomes an advertiser, simply because he has to.

A classic commercial pattern begins to emerge. People like what he has for sale. They consume it in quantity, and he prospers. But his early prosperity is limited by the restrictions of the market he serves. Awareness of this fact leads him to conclude that he can make more money by selling his product to more people in more places. To this end he expands distribution, which requires him also to extend the reach of his advertising.

In the meanwhile, however, something else is going on that is equally inescapable. Another entrepreneur has observed his success and has undertaken to make and sell an imitation of the product, or one very much like it. At some point the two competitive brands are preordained to collide head-on. When this happens, each of the entrepreneurs goes to work as hard as he knows how to get the lion's share of the sales. Moreover, the second marketer—not unlike the first—also relies on advertising as the least expensive, most efficient way to persuade the buying public to choose his product instead of his competitor's.

Both entrepreneurs have turned to advertising because there is no other method available by which to reach so large a number of people, so often, at so few cents per person. And it goes without saying that the more universal the appeal of the product, and the more likely it is to be found in self-service retail outlets, the more effective and efficient advertising becomes.

At the same time, of course, the advertising itself also becomes highly competitive. It may be done well or badly, in good taste or bad. But it is necessary that it be done—because this is the way our system operates. The fact is that as long as we have competitive enterprises, and as long as entrepreneurs want to profit from them, advertising will always be an essential function of the business scene—along with production, packaging, distribution, sales, accounting, and all the other business activities.

There is another area of confused thinking that should be identified and clarified. It is this: there is a lively body of opinion that objects to advertising in support of products that are thought to be harmful or undesirable. For example, tobacco products are said to be bad for you, therefore tobacco advertising is wicked. In discussions of this kind, and in legislative enactments as well, advertising becomes the culprit instead of the advertiser who employs it. On the other hand, a dispassionate observer might well come to the conclusion that the way to keep people from smoking cigarettes is to force the manufacturers to discontinue making them rather than to crack down on the advertising of them. The moral here, if there is one, would seem to be that when we feel like denouncing advertising we should attempt to identify the nature of our objection. Is it to the advertising, or is it to the advertiser who uses it and the purpose for which it is used?

You might want to think of it this way: Is the hammer used to build a house a good hammer, and the one used to beat someone's brains out a bad one? Or does the problem lie with the set of mind of the user and the purpose for which he uses the tool? The analogy is perfectly valid, and the distinction is important.

THIS IS ADVERTISING

In any event, you will make up your own mind about the part that highly competitive product advertising plays in relation to our higher social aspirations. And it may be interesting to note that many advertising agencies have addressed themselves to the same concern. Some will not take on a tobacco account; some will not work for a distillery; many will not accept a political candidate as a client (no matter what his party affiliation). Others have more broadly stated policies which boil down to refusing to do any advertising for any client if the agency believes what he wants to do or say is not in the best interest of society.

On the other side of the coin, advertisers and agencies and media owners combine annually to donate large quantities of time, money, effort, and space to a considerable list of advertising projects in the public interest. For the most part, these are administered through an organization called the Advertising Council. The Council has been in operation for over 30 years. It is a private non-profit corporation, supported solely by American business and the advertising and communications industries. It works in conjunction with the American Association of Advertising Agencies. Each project is assigned to a separate agency which develops the advertising at its own expense.

The Council's operating budget—contributed by the member companies—runs over $725,000 annually, and the estimated value of the advertising placed through it was $525,000,-000 as of the end of the fiscal year in June of 1973. That is a lot of money spent on the side of the angels ! The roster of the causes supported by this effort in the last year is reasonably typical of any year's list. It includes:
- Volunteers for ACTION
- Aid to Higher Education
- American Red Cross
- Consumer Information (for the Council of Better Business Bureaus)
- Continue Your Education
- Cost of Living Campaign (How to Help Combat Inflation)
- Drug Abuse Information

- Food, Nutrition, and Health
- Forest Fire Prevention
- Help Prevent Crime
- Help Fight Pollution
- Jobs for Veterans
- Support Minority Business Enterprise
- JOBS Program
- Planned Parenthood/World Population
- Rehabilitation of the Handicapped
- Promotion of Religion in American Life
- Support for Technical Training (Department of H.E.W.)
- Traffic Safety
- United Community Campaigns
- United Negro College Fund
- U.S. Savings Bonds
- V.D. Awareness Campaign

(An up-to-date list of current projects—each with a short description—can be obtained from the Advertising Council, 825 Third Ave., New York, N.Y., 10022.)

Additionally, there is a long list of charities that use advertising to educate people about health and related problems—or to plead for contributions to research or remedial activities. No one who watches television should have any trouble spotting a half-dozen different appeals of this kind every week.

Finally, almost every advertising agency of any size is likely to have one or two pet charitable, educational or civic projects which it helps support by preparing and placing advertising for free.

It would be interesting to be able to compute the precise number of dollars that are spent on activities of this kind each year. Unfortunately, such figures are not available. However, it is probably conservative to assume that the annual investment in all these appeals approximates one-quarter billion dollars.

It becomes clear that advertising is a necessary and integral part of our complex, modern industrial society; that much of it is used as a force for good, although some of it undoubtedly is not; and that however it is used it is here to stay, because our type of society cannot do without it.

III   REGULATION

Back in the bad old days when advertising was beginning to become a really important factor in our way of doing business there were those whose interest in making a buck exceeded their concern for truth and probity. (Or else, their respect for the truth was so great that they used it sparingly.) The result was a proliferation of claims for a variety of products that were good for whatever ailed you, regardless of what the real problem may have been. Examples of these offerings can be found in almost any periodical of the latter nineteenth century.

As time went on these excesses diminished almost to the vanishing point. Their virtual disappearance was attributable to the growth of social consciousness, and also to the discovery that the net effect of promoting an unsatisfactory product merely served to alert an increasingly large number of people to the fact that it was no good.

Growth in social consciousness led to the development of a variety of purifying agents—a development that is still going on. The result is that we now have a very large and complicated body of laws, regulations, principles and codes aimed at protecting the public from dishonest, fraudulent, and misleading claims. These safeguards range from the standards that the members of the American Association of Advertising Agencies agree to follow as a condition of membership, to various state and federal consumer protection agencies.

These restraints on deception are divided between voluntary controls and governmental regulations. In the voluntary category are such things as the standards of the AAAA's; the National Advertising Review Board (which operates in conjunction with the Council of Better Business Bureaus to cause advertisers to withdraw advertising that is considered to be misleading, or in some other way inappropriate or improper); the code of the National Association of Broadcasters which sets rules to guide radio and television stations about what is considered acceptable and unacceptable advertising to go out over the air; and the standards that every publisher sets for his own publications. Many of the latter are very strict.

Governmental regulation is provided in part by legislative action (as in the case of the ban on cigarette advertising on television), and to an even greater extent by the judgments and proclamations of such administrative agencies as the FTC, and the FCC, the FDA, and many more. The overall thrust of what these agencies are trying to do is all for the good. At this writing, however, they are not always consistent and are hardly ever predictable. This is troublesome to many advertisers because they cannot be sure of what is currently permissible phrasing of a claim and what is not. This is not surprising, however, as it is representative of the kinds of problems that usually accompany the development of a new body of laws and legal precedents.

Each of us will have to make up his own mind as to whether the free forces of the market place provide more effective controls than even an enlightened bureaucrat's ideas of what it is safe to say to a presumably gullible and uninformed public. Currently, this is an area of considerable disagreement. And it is not likely to be settled for a long time, although a betting man would certainly give odds on the growth of the consumer protection movement.

IV ECONOMIC FORCE OF ADVERTISING

It is clear that advertising is an economic force; that it plays an important part in the conduct of business in this and other countries (now it is being used even in Russia); and that it provides an efficient means of transmitting information about a great variety of subjects and products. What is not equally clear is how many economic "G's" it exerts. Nevertheless, as in the case of its effect or impact on society, a great deal has been written on the subject.

Much of this writing purports to be scholarly, with suitable footnotes and cross references. Most of it can reasonably be accused of being turgid, labored and contrived. No small amount is motivated by an obvious prejudice for or against advertising—with its practitioners voting heavily in favor, and segments of the intellectual community, for the most part, voting "Nay."

No attempt will be made here to produce a lengthy disquisition on this matter. To do so would be to go beyond the scope of this volume, and to strain the good nature of this observer as well. Extensive reading of source material on this subject leads to the conviction that true measurement of advertising's economic force or contribution is not possible at this stage of our commercial history. There are just two many "ifs," "ands," and "buts;" too many unprovable assumptions; and too many moot conclusions.

THIS IS ADVERTISING

It may seem strange that such is the case. But it is safe to say an explanation is to be found in the fact that, to date, no one has been able to perfect a technique for measuring the effects of advertising, or arrive at an explanation of precisely how it works. And without such scientific understanding and calibration as a basic premise, every broad conclusion with respect to its overall effects can only be dubious at best, and spurious at worst. Accordingly, the purpose here will be limited to recording some of the obvious and readily recognizable contributions that advertising makes to our economy, and to identifying some of the factors and viewpoints likely to be encountered in considerations of just how much force it does exert.

This chapter started with the bald statement that advertising is an economic force, which is a true statement even if the extent of that force is not easily measurable. The reason is empirical—both experience and history say so. Those who sell goods or services have demonstrated to their own satisfaction year in and year out that they need to advertise in order to conduct their businesses profitably. (Incidentally, this is not a new idea. It has been recorded that a rudimentary form of advertising took place in Pompeii in the first century A.D. Moreover, the Constitution of the United States was first published in *"The Pennsylvania Packet and Daily Advertiser"* (No. 2690 in 1776). Conversely, there are some classic cases of once aggressively advertised products that were leaders, or among the leaders, in their fields for many years and which have since fallen by the wayside. They disappeared from the marketplace largely as a result of deliberate decisions to discontinue advertising them. Among them are:

Force cereal.
Pears Soap—which led all other soaps combined.
Sappolio Cleanser—which was number one for 30 years.
Sweet Caporals, and Fatimas—which together controlled the
    early cigarette market.
Djer-Kiss—perfumes and cosmetics.
Gold Dust Cleanser.
Fairy Soap.

Now other brands whose names are easier to call to mind lead in these same fields. There are other examples as well, but these should serve to make the point without laboring it.

As a measure of the faith the commercial community has in advertising, two sets of statistics are worth recording. The first is that almost $26,000,000,000 (twenty-six billion) was spent in advertising in the U.S.A. in 1973. This was about two and a half billion dollars more than was spent the preceding year.

The other is that advertising expenditures tend to grow in almost direct proportion to our Gross National Product. Here is how the relationship looked over the last five years:

	Gross National Product	U.S. Advertising Expenditures	Advertising as a percent of G.N.P.
	(in billions of dollars)		
1973	$1,334.0	$25.8	1.9%
1972	$1,155.2	$23.1	2.7%
1971	$1,055.5	$20.8	1.9%
1970	$ 977.1	$19.6	2.0%
1969	$ 930.3	$19.5	2.1%

The above figures are not intended to indicate that the increase in advertising expenditures necessarily *caused* the Gross National Product to grow as it did (although some advertising extremists would have us think so). The figures do show, however, that these expenditures are an integral component of our economy and that their performance is consistent with that of other indices.

(Incidentally, in 1973 almost exactly half of this advertising volume was placed through advertising agencies—$12.9 billion.)

THIS IS ADVERTISING

Another indicator of the economic importance of advertising may be found in the case of some categories of successful low-cost, high-frequency-of-purchase items, in which the cost of advertising sometimes represents as much as one-third of the total marketing expense. If this percentage seems excessive, it should be remembered that no successful businessman spends more on his advertising than he thinks he has to. Expenditures of this magnitude are committed repeatedly only because they are needed to ensure the sale of enough product, whatever it may be, to keep the company that makes it in business, at a profit.

It should be acknowledged, however, that the economic effect of advertising varies widely, depending on the kind of product it is asked to support. At one end of the scale are things like locomotives and heavy industrial equipment. With respect to the sale of these, advertising's contributions are of relatively less importance. But at the other end are the so-called "package goods" items—like soap, cereals, health and beauty aids—to whose sales advertising is vital. Moreover, there are products and services that are sold only through the mail. For these, advertising is an absolute essential.

Regardless of the total economic contribution that advertising makes, there are known facts about the business which help to reveal its dimensions. Already it has been shown that huge sums of money are spent on advertising yearly. Curiously, however, less than one-tenth of one percent of the population works at it—the most recent estimates being that some 200,000 people are engaged in it; that roughly 20,000 newcomers enter it every year in some capacity, and only a small percentage of these go to work for advertising agencies.

According to the American Association of Advertising Agencies, there are 5,700 advertising agencies in the United States. For the most part, they are concentrated in the large cities. Agency openings for college or B-school graduates are quite limited, however. The AAAA's estimates that there are only 800 to 1,000 such openings each year—which makes for a fairly select group, smaller than the graduating class of almost any major educational institution you can think of. As a benchmark for comparison, we turn out roughly 8,900 new doctors, and 18,000 new lawyers annually.

Aside from the effect of the expenditure of so much money on the sale of goods and services, the leverage those dollars exert is readily apparent in its effect on television, radio, newspapers and magazines; for without advertising there would be no such thing as free TV or radio. Both of these channels of entertainment and information are totally supported by advertising revenues. They have no other source of income. The one exception is the National Educational Television network which is partially supported by government grants and partially by individual and corporate contributions. If you live in an area that has a N.E.T. station you may know how it has to scrounge for funds to keep going.

The case of magazines and newspapers is not quite so extreme, although both these media are made possible *in their current form* by the advertising they carry. Without it they could not continue to provide the wire services, reporters, editors, columnists, photographers, staff workers and others, unless the reading public was willing to pay a substantially greater price per copy. The demise of two weekly magazines illustrate this. The *Saturday Evening Post* and *Life* were forced to discontinue publication because their advertising revenues fell below the level necessary to sustain them, even after they had raised their subscription and single copy prices as high as their readers would stand.

The typical newspaper would have to sell for at least 50 to 60 cents a copy, instead of 10 to 15 cents, to preserve its present character, and it seems highly improbable that many people would be able or willing to pay that much for a paper every day.

Finally, a great many people actually like advertising and find it hard to get along without it. Only a couple of examples are needed to make the point. Some years ago a group of major merchants in Philadelphia decided to boycott one of the city's leading newspapers because of a dispute over rates charged by it. They discontinued buying advertising space, with the result that the paper's circulation declined by half. It did not recover until the argument was settled and its readers could once again count on seeing regularly what all the local stores had to offer.

Any time there is a protracted strike of all the newspapers, or of the only one in some cities, we see dramatic evidence of this. When that happens most of the retailers print and distribute flyers or giveaways. Not because they want to be in the publishing business, but because their customers want to know what can be bought, where it can be bought, and what it will cost. So, advertising makes its presence felt in many ways and probably exerts an economic force that is greatly disproportionate to the relatively small number of people engaged in it. A good way to form a personal idea of its overall significance is to assume that after today there will be no more advertising of any kind, ever. Contemplating *all* the changes that would then take place, you will find yourself truly imagining the unimaginable.

V   FORMS AND FUNCTIONS

We have said that advertising is a "method of mass communication characterized by economy, speed, control and responsibility" and that such a definition seems sufficiently flexible to accommodate all the necessary assignments it is asked to carry out.

For purposes of further clarification, most advertising vehicles or media are broadly identified as national, regional, or local. Thus *Newsweek* is a national medium, and a low-powered radio station is a local one. At the same time some media—notably television—are national when a full network is used, regional when an advertiser uses a group of selected stations, and local when only one station is used.

So now let us review the variety of forms that advertising assumes, with a brief comment on the major characteristics of each.

Television. The most visible, the most compelling, and certainly the most controversial medium that we see. As noted, it can be used in several ways. Network TV is used to promote products or services that have nationwide distribution, and that generally speaking fit the pocketbooks of almost everybody. Network TV is used also to broadcast messages about subjects of broad national interest or concern; or to carry to as many people as possible statements having to do with what some company is, or does, or stands for, or wants to be known for. Regional or local TV is used for the same purposes on a more limited scale.

Moreover, it is being increasingly used locally by such retailers as supermarkets, department stores, discount outlets, and automobile dealers—to name only a few. It is also useful to many locally distributed items of common general consumption, like bread and beer, as well as for local charitable and civic causes.

The great bulk of TV advertising is in the form of 30-second spots, now frequently in piggy-back configuration; that is, two or more commercials in succession. Reminder messages and announcements of "upcoming" programs also appear in 10- and 20-second lengths. These usually are the "station breaks" that come between the end of one program and the beginning of another. Less usual are commercials of 60-seconds or longer.

For the most part, the networks produce the shows that appear on TV or buy them from independent producers or "packagers" who develop, among other programs, many of the quiz shows on the air. In a few cases, advertisers have a hand in developing programs of their own which they believe will provide exactly the right setting for their advertising. There is another category of programs—referred to as "specials" or "spectaculars"—which usually run from one to two hours in length. Within these the 60-second, two-minute, or even three-minute commercials are most likely to be found.

Although most television programming and advertising is designed to attract the broadest possible audience, some programs are specifically tailored to appeal to audiences that are both somewhat smaller and more selective. For instance, golf and tennis telecasts are thought to attract viewers who are predominantly male and whose income, educational, and managerial levels are substantially above average. The products customarily advertised on such broadcasts are those to which such viewers presumably have a very high level of sensitivity, such as equipment associated with those sports or expensive items of office equipment or services.

In 1973 about 19% of all advertising dollars were spent in television; about two-thirds in network; and one-third in spot.

Radio. Of all media available to advertisers, radio broadcasts reach the most people—the biggest mass audiences—and in the greatest number of places and circumstances. The vast majority of homes in this country have two or more radio sets, and on top of that there are all the car radios and boat radios, not to mention the number of portables that are now being carried and listened to by people on foot.

In recognition of this, radio is used by national advertisers to promote goods and services that are widely purchased. Locally, pretty much the same thing is true. Automobile dealers and discount stores are big users of radio; whereas Tiffany's, for example, is not.

There are only a few network radio programs on the air now, although before television they were as common as today's TV network shows. Consequently, most advertisers who use radio for national coverage do so by buying spots on a city-by-city, station-by-station basis.

As with television there are some slightly more selective uses of radio. Maybe the prime example is in the early morning and late afternoon when people are driving to and from work—called "drive time" in the trade. At these times advertisers with products likely to appeal to men are heavy users of the medium. Gasoline, tires, batteries, new and used cars, airline departures, and messages encouraging safe driving or urging people not to drink and drive are prominent during these periods.

The programming practices of the individual stations are designed to make them particularly attractive to various ethnic groups or to identifiable age groups. The kinds of products advertised on such stations are those that are likely to appeal to the tastes of such segments of the public.

Radio expenditures account for 2% of all advertising dollars, and less than 20% of that is in network advertising.

THIS IS ADVERTISING

All licensed commercial television and radio stations are required by law to provide free time for messages in the public interest. Each must keep a log that records how many were aired and at what times of the day or night. Many of these, of course, are those sponsored by the Advertising Council.

Newspapers. This category has a number of well-known components: dailies, weeklies, Sundays, Sunday supplements, comics, and other special sections. Taken as a whole, however, newspapers are true mass media with no particular appeal to any one segment of the population, although there are two notable exceptions in general circulation: *The Wall Street Journal* and *The Christian Science Monitor.* There is a substantial number of ethnic and foreign language newspapers as well.

Newspapers are *the* timely local medium, and probably as much as 80% of the advertising appearing in them is placed by local businesses, even though the Sunday supplements and comics are used extensively by advertisers whose products are sold in and around major cities all over the country.

Where one radio station relies on hard rock to attract listeners and another on classical music, newspapers achieve somewhat the same result through their different sections and departments. Advertising is placed in those sections where it fits best—new bond issues in the financial pages, cake mixes in the women's section, houses for sale in the real estate section, children's products like candy bars in the Sunday comics (despite the fact that many more adults than children read the comics), and so on.

More dollars are spent in newspaper advertising than in any other medium. They account for 42% of the total.

Magazines. For the most part, magazines are a very selective medium. Each is edited to appeal to the needs, interests or tastes of a particular segment of the population. Only the *Reader's Digest* can be described accurately as a simon-pure "general" magazine. The immensely popular *TV Guide* is oriented towards people with a deep interest in television; *Time* and *Newsweek* are current events magazines; *Sports Illustrated, Science Illustrated* and *Gourmet*—as their names indicate—are even more sharply focused, and so it goes.

In the advertising business, periodicals like the above are called consumer magazines, and even more specialized ones are put in the category of "trade" papers. Examples are publications like *Advertising Age, Automotive News,* and *Casket and Sunnyside* (the journal of the mortuary trade). All these, and their number is legion, are designed to provide information and opinions about various specialized fields of endeavor.

Almost all magazines circulate nationally and consequently carry advertising for items that are available nationally. Increasingly, however, they also carry advertising which may appear only in one or more local, state or regional editions of the magazine. There is also a growing number of very good ones that are edited solely for local or regional tastes and interests. These bear descriptive titles like *New York* and *Philadelphia Magazine* and carry advertising for local enterprises.

There is a large body of available information about the demographics of the readers of successful magazines; that is, their ages, incomes, educational levels, occupations, residences (owned or rented), buying habits, car ownership, etc. In fact, a few magazines sell advertising space in special editions that are bought and read by only the uppermost end of the demographic scale. The makers of the most luxurious cars, the most expensive liquors, the most precious jewelry, and other comparable luxury items advertise in these special editions.

Of total advertising expenditures, 13% goes into this category—about 60% of that in consumer magazines and the other 40% in trade papers.

<u>Outdoor.</u> This takes essentially two forms. These are 24-sheet posters, commonly known as billboards, and painted spectacular displays that are almost always lighted and often are animated in some manner. Normally, 24-sheet posters are replaced

with new paper every month, while painted boards remain un-changed for from three to twelve months.

This medium is obviously aimed at the whole population and makes no pretense of being selective. It must be bought on a city-by-city basis as there is no national network. Most often it is used by national advertisers to carry short reminder messages in support of low-cost, frequently purchased products like soft drinks, beer, tobacco products and chewing gum. It is widely used also by automobile manufacturers at the time of new model introductions, the theory being that this is a good way to show what the new cars look like, almost life-sized.

Local advertisers use outdoor for the same kinds of products and also for services having widespread local appeal. A typical example of the latter would be bank Christmas club savings ac-counts.

A sub-category of this medium is the smaller posters of varying dimensions found in airline and bus terminals, and in railroad stations. These are used by advertisers whose products relate to the activities of most of the people passing by them. Ex-amples range from reminders to call ahead or home by long-distance, to travel resort promotion, and to a very substantial amount of space donated to worthy causes of the kind supported by the Advertising Council.

In all, outdoor expenditures represent about 2% of total advertising dollars.

Direct mail. This second largest dollar category of adver-tising comes in many forms. At one end of the scale are the mailings addressed to "Occupant," and at the other are highly personalized letters inscribed to the recipient and bearing a real or facsimile signature.

Thanks to computerization and other sophisticated techni-ques for developing mailing lists, direct mail is the most selective communications medium there is. Its addressee can be picked out by such diverse criteria as postal zone residence, annual incomes of over $50,000, season ticket-holders to cultural or sporting events, and an almost endless list of other controlling factors. It can be sent to any number of people, from one to several millions. Both local and national advertisers use it to sell almost everything—from one-dollar subscriptions to the local "Little League" to a set of the "100 Great Books of All Time" at $30.25 each, plus local taxes and shipping charges.

It is especially attractive to many advertisers because, despite the fact that it is an expensive way to communicate (in relation to the other major media) in many cases its payout is the most truly measurable of that of any type of advertising. As a result of continuous testing of the lists of target recipients and the selling appeals used, the response to new campaigns can often be predicted with surprising accuracy.

In form, direct mail can consist of almost anything, but most common are letters, postcards, envelope stuffers, subscription cards in magazines, booklets and brochures, and various kinds of attention-getting inexpensive novelties.

In dollars it represents about 21% of the total amount spent in media for which there are money measurements.

Miscellaneous. There is a handful of highly specialized and relatively restricted forms of advertising that should also be identified to complete the list. Although there are no truly reliable estimates of the advertising dollars spent in these sub-media, it is safe to say that the amount is insignificant in relation to the total. Nevertheless, here they are.

Car Cards. Another mass medium found in bus, trolley, subway and commuter train cars. Offshoots of these are signs on the outside of buses and on the roofs or trunks of taxis.

Dioramas and displays. In airports and train stations and used principally to advertise airlines, luggage, credit cards and other things having to do with travel.

Matchbook covers. Advertising is sold on these for distribution nationally, regionally, or locally.

THIS IS ADVERTISING

Skywriting and airborne banners. Available to advertisers who think they have value, but very little is known about the numbers of people who pay attention to them or are motivated by them. They are not often used. Occasionally though, a banner can be seen over a crowded football stadium urging the coach to get out of town.

Shoppers. This is the trade name for tabloid-size free giveaways; printed on newsprint; hand delivered to houses and apartments; and usually listing specially priced drug, grocery, or general merchandise items. These are occasionally employed by local merchants for limited local distribution.

Sound trucks. These horrifying machines seem to be coming into use more and more—particularly those trailing billboard-sized signs. They usually require municipal licensing and are used largely to advertise political candidates, local restaurants, movies, or race tracks.

Generally speaking, there are three parties involved in the development and execution of advertising for nationally distributed products. They are the advertisers, the advertising agencies, and the media available for the assignment. The main burden of this book will be devoted to the functions and structure of advertising agencies; the opportunities they present; and the kind of people they attract. To complete the record, however, it will also include brief sketches of the advertising jobs and responsibilities in the advertisers' organizations and in the media operations.

VI

THE PEOPLE IN AN ADVERTISING AGENCY

What are agency people like? What kind of person is likely to enjoy the agency business and to do well in it?

These are the key questions of anyone who is interested in getting into the business. It is essential that the aspiring agency man or woman understands, truly comprehends, the answers and can realistically assess his or her capabilities and aptitude for an agency career. Let us see if we can help.

What are agency people like? To begin with, as with men and women in other lines of endeavor, they come in assorted sizes, shapes, hues, talents, backgrounds, philosophies, likes and dislikes, and other human traits and characteristics. There is no stereotype, no man in a gray flannel suit, nor should there be. The best agencies have the greatest diversity of talents and outlooks. So much so that one distinguished practitioner has described his agency as being more of a menagerie than an organization. He said it with pride and affection because his agency is notably successful, widely respected, and highly regarded as a place to work.

But although agency people are a heterogeneous lot, all are likely to be very bright and to have at least these common characteristics—interest, imagination, initiative, energy, and a well-developed competitive instinct. As related to the agency business, these characteristics require some explanation.

Interest means the natural and normal interest in the immediate job or assignment, and the affairs and well-being of the agency and its clients. All of that is obvious. As used here, however, it also means a lively interest in almost everything else under the sun. Maybe a good synonym would be "curiosity"—curiosity about people and what makes them tick; curiosity about both our physical and socio-economic environment; curiosity about political and governmental trends and developments; curiosity about new (and old) products and services; curiosity about art, books, theater, fashions, food, drink, manufacturing processes and methods of distribution; and most particularly, curiosity about trends in life styles and behavioral patterns, and about attitudes that affect purchasing habits and the buyer-seller relationship. Good advertising people, like good doctors and good lawyers, must be devoted to continuing self renewal, to educating and re-educating themselves constantly.

Imagination means the ability to relate seemingly unrelated facts, or to "recombine former experiences" as a way of arriving at new ideas and of meeting and resolving difficulties. It means not only the ability to create new ideas but also the ability to recognize, evaluate and improve on other people's thinking and ideas. The use of imagination should help in arriving at practical, realistic solutions to advertising and marketing problems. And almost all the best advertising men and women nourish their imaginative powers through the ongoing educational process already mentioned.

Initiative. The dictionary defines "initiative" as: "readiness and ability in originating action," and as taking action as a result of "one's personal responsible decision." In order to do well in the advertising agency world it is essential that a person qualify in exactly those terms. In the vernacular, unless you are a self-starter the agency business is not for you.

Energy, for our purposes here, means a combination of willingness to put in long hours on frequent occasions and the stamina to do so. The advertising business has no monopoly on energy as an ingredient of success, but it is well to remember two things. First, an agency performs a service. It and the people in it work for somebody else (the client) and must be prepared to accept and execute many, often difficult, assignments on very short notice. Second, as has been noted, there are no precise, widely accepted measurements of how advertising works, which tends to make it more of an art than a science. This being so, there are, inevitably, differences of opinion about what is or is not a good advertisement or advertising campaign. Thus, whenever the advertiser is convinced that his agency has presented him with advertising that is not good, it is back to the drawing board at the agency—with time running out and energy at a premium.

Competitive instinct means having a high level of desire for the success of one's clients and their products which the agency advertises. It also means having great determination to develop outstanding advertising—more exciting and effective than that being done by any other agency. All business is competitive, of course. But perhaps none is more so than the agency business—probably because today the greatest opportunities for agency growth and profitability come from securing new accounts that were formerly served by other agencies. Unlike lawyers and accountants, whose clients tend to desert them infrequently and without fanfare, agency-client relationships are *relatively* short-lived. Moreover, losses and acquisitions are widely reported in advertising trade publications and major city newspapers, much like a running competitive scorecard that regularly records entries in the won and lost columns. Successful advertising people have to accept this climate, and most of them thrive on it.

What kind of a person is likely to enjoy the agency business and to do well in it? Certainly people who are interested (or curious), imaginative, self-starters, energetic and competitive, but there are other attributes that are useful as well. The principal ones must include the following:

Personal integrity. It is true, of course, that all successful business and human relationships depend on the integrity of the people involved. In the advertising agency business, however, there are two characteristic conditions that place a premium on integrity. The first is that many dealings and arrangements with clients and colleagues are done on the basis of oral agreements and these must always be honored scrupulously. Also, the initial negotiations in the purchase of radio and television time are done orally, and a person who does not live up to his word does not last long in the business.

The second and possibly less obvious requirement for integrity is of a slightly different kind. For the most part clients employ agencies to do more than simply make advertisements. They are also expected to develop advertising plans and recommendations which will operate to the greatest benefit of their clients, and much time, analysis, and deliberation go into such development. But, since advertising is not a precise science, judgment always plays a leading role in the final proposals that the agency makes. And a first-class agency man or woman must be prepared to support his or her beliefs with conviction and tactful determination in the face of client questioning, or even outright disagreement. It is in this recurrent situation that both self-respect and self-preservation often call for a high degree of integrity. Simply stated, to be effective and successful you have to believe and to be willing to support your belief.

An urge for diversity. One of the greatest pleasures for most advertising people comes from the fact that each assignment or problem is likely to be different from all the rest and distinct from the last. Furthermore, in the course of an advertising career the practitioner will be exposed to, learn about, become familiar with, and work with a variety of businesses—each with unique characteristics, concerns, appeals to consumers (en masse or in smaller selective segments), channels of distribution, and trade practices and traditions. Advertising is not for those who seek the comfortable groove or the security-blanket of repetitive chores.

Team spirit. With rare exceptions, agency recommendations are an amalgam of ideas and contributions of many people specializing in different functions. The business is satisfying and rewarding, therefore, only for the person who is enthusiastic about the group of which he is a member and the quality of its collective output. Interestingly enough, however, it is the nature of agency team operation to encourage each individual to make his own valuable contribution—to do his own thing. Consequently, being part of a team actually accents the individual's participation rather than detracting from it. For many this is the best of both possible worlds.

Respect for the views of others. This asset is closely allied to team spirit. In fact, the two are inseparable in the internal workings of an agency. Moreover, it is clear that clients are entitled to their own views, and even when they differ sharply from those of the agency they demand respect, attention, understanding and, not infrequently, accommodation. A wise old agency man once put it in a nutshell. Commenting on some colleague's unwillingness to listen to an advertiser's viewpoint, he asked: "How come we have all the brains, and the client has all the money?"

Ability to communicate. It should be readily apparent from much of the foregoing that such ability, or facility, is an essential ingredient of the person wishing to make a career in an advertising agency. Ideas are hard enough to deal with under any circumstances, but without clear comprehensible communication (both oral and written) many disasters can confidently be expected. Conversely, it is equally important to be able and willing to listen to what others are saying and to decipher what they mean by it. This is a talent that can be perfected through practice, but in this business "they who have ears but hear not" are doomed.

A sense of humor. The advertising agency business is not always an easy one. No one enjoys hearing his brain-child systematically dismembered or criticized to extinction. But it happens, because not all judgments are as sound as others, not all ideas as good as others (and some are very bad indeed). Furthermore, it happens to everyone, and when it happens to you, you have to be able to laugh it off, or at least to be able to grin and bear it. People being what they are, in an advertising environment the ridiculous is likely to be encountered more often than the sublime, and over the long haul a sense of humor is essential to the agency person's recuperative powers, health, and euphoria.

VII WHAT AN ADVERTISING AGENCY IS

Maybe the best way to start describing an agency is to begin with a very brief history of one that came into being in 1869. At that time there were all kinds of newspapers and magazines (most of them very small by modern standards) scattered all over the country, as there are now. All were eager to sell space in their publications to advertisers, then as now. But they had a problem: how were they to identify all the potential advertisers and then persuade them to advertise in their periodicals? They found the answer by appointing "advertising agents" who were in fact salesmen for the publishers, and thus publishers' agents rather than advertisers' agents. These agents were compensated by allowing them a percentage (usually 15%) of the cost of the space they sold.

In those days the business practices of the agents appear to have been patterned after those of the oriental bazaars; the doctrine of *caveat emptor* was supreme. Little by little, however, such men as Ayer and Thompson, recognizing the need for ethical practices and standards, cleaned the business up and put it on a more professional basis. And in doing so they changed their agencies' allegiance from publisher to advertiser. They began to work for the advertiser as his agent, but their compensation continued to come from the media as before. And for the most part, it still does.

At first the agents merely bought space for their clients; then they offered help in writing and designing the advertising to go in that space; and subsequently, as the trade became more sophisticated, they responded to other emerging needs of their clients until the typical present-day agency structure was reached. It was an evolutionary process. There was no preconceived plan or grand design. This fact explains any apparent anachronisms in today's practices.

(If you have further interest in the historical development of the agency business in this country, *The History of an Advertising Agency* by Harvard Professor Ralph M. Hower, Harvard University Press, Cambridge, Mass., is highly recommended.)

In any event, modern agencies represent the interests of their clients and place their advertisements in whatever media are thought to be best suited to the client's purposes. The most substantial agencies now represent companies whose business is regional or national and who believe that their agencies can provide two things they need and want. The first of these are the services of a collection of professional advertising people with a variety of skills and experience, at a cost lower than that which the advertiser would have to pay to maintain a similar staff. The second is the objectivity that an independent organization can bring to the identification of the advertiser's problems and opportunities, and to the development of programs designed to help solve the one and take advantage of the other.

Smaller local companies often employ agencies as well, although in many such instances for limited services only.

The large-budget advertisers who do not use agencies are for the most part large local retailers, like department stores and supermarkets, which sell a wide range of products—many bearing national brands—and whose offer is predominantly price and availability. These organizations have their own fully-staffed internal advertising departments.

On the other hand, a few retail giants like Sears and Penney, who have stores all over the country, do employ agencies to advertise their own nationally sold lines of merchandise such as tires, batteries, shoes, apparel, and appliances.

It has been noted that agencies get paid for their work largely by retaining a percentage of the cost of the space or time bought from the media for their clients' advertising. And, as we have seen, the reason is historical. It works this way. One unit of space in a publication or of time on the air is worth, say, $1,000. The agency contracts for it for its client. The medium makes out a bill for the full amount and sends it to the agency, which in turn sends a similar invoice to the client. The client sends the agency $1,000, and the agency then normally pays the medium $850, retaining $150 (15%) as its commission for its services. This customary arrangement is known as the "commission system," and most of the client-agency-media transactions are conducted on this basis.

The remaining small percentage of such transactions are carried out on a fee basis. Paid by the client to the agency, the fee covers the agency's manpower, traveling and other operating expenses, plus a reasonable profit. Lawyers and accountants are compensated for their services in the same way.

In recent years there has been a noisy but inconclusive debate about the pros and cons of the commission system versus the fee system. Those on the side of commissions are small advertisers for whom fee payments would likely represent substantially increased costs, and agencies having clients who spend enormous sums against a relatively small number of commercials or printed advertisements each year. On the fee side are some of the "large budget/few ads" advertisers and those agencies which do a lot of work for clients with small budgets. And, quite obviously, the same agency can be on both sides of the fence for economic reasons.

Theoretically it seems apparent that if the whole business were starting from scratch today, agencies would be compensated only by fees. Nevertheless, the commission system is still the basis upon which most of the business is done.

It should be recorded that in part agencies are compensated also by charging an override, or commission, on materials and services bought from outside suppliers or subcontractors—like artists, photographers, printers, engravers, film producers and recording studios. The usual add-on is 17.65% and it is needed to defray the internal costs of managing and arranging these important details. Additionally, fees are charged for such non-advertising activities as publicity and public relations services, speech writing, sales promotion work, staging and conducting sales meetings, and the like.

Industry figures indicate that the bigger the agency the greater the percentage of revenue from commissions and the smaller the percentage from fees for special services. It is estimated that the largest agencies get something like 80% to 85% of their income from commissions on space and time, about 10% to 15% from add-ons to suppliers invoices, and maybe 5% from special fees. The figures for smaller agencies are roughly 60%, 25%, and 15%, respectively. The difference reflects the fact that the small agencies—typically serving low budget advertisers—cannot make a living by preparing advertising to run in publications of limited circulation and low cost, and on local TV and radio stations on which time is inexpensive. (It requires as much time and effort to write and design an advertisement for a country weekly as for the *New York Times.*) So they must have additional fee income in order to meet their payrolls.

Now, what does an agency do to justify the money it takes in regardless of the method of its compensation?

First, its primary responsibility lies in planning, creating and preparing, and placing advertising in one or more media on behalf of its clients. In order to carry out these assignments professionally and successfully, it must be structured to perform certain basic functions. They follow.

Agency management. As in any other business, someone has to be in charge—someone who can provide the necessary leadership, make the final management decisions, and see that the agency's policies are carried out. In larger agencies, policies are usually established by a Board of Directors and executed by a

Chief Executive Officer, who may have the title either of Chairman of the Board or of President. In smaller agencies, the policy-making function is often discharged by the principal owner, who is likely also to be the Chief Executive.

Account management. The job of keeping in touch and in tune with the client; of representing his views to the rest of the agency; and of presenting the agency's views, recommendations and advertising to him is charged to Account Management Supervisors, Account Supervisors, and Account Executives.

Creative services. Here is where the broadcast commercials and print advertisements are made by a combination of writers, artists, TV commercial producers and other specialists as they may be needed. In some agencies other activities like fashion coordination or casting and talent direction also fall into this category.

Traffic control. This difficult assignment is to make sure that all the necessary printing and reproduction materials, electrical transcriptions for radio spots, film and tapes for television commercials are prepared, submitted to the client for his approval, and furnished to the various media in time to meet their established deadlines.

Media services. Media specialists select the form of medium to be used and the individual stations, networks, newspapers, or magazines best suited to the objectives of the advertising; negotiate for and order television and radio spot availabilities; and contract for and order print space.

Research. This activity is organized differently from agency to agency, but it generally divides into a market research section which investigates goings-on in the marketplace (with particular emphasis on consumer characteristics, attitudes, and behavior) and a copy research section which tests the effectiveness of various copy approaches, appeals, and techniques.

Finance and administration. This is sort of a catch-all function that usually combines personnel, office management (procedures and systems), payroll, billing and paying bills, accounting, and management of the agency's finances.

New business. The growth of every agency rests on its success in attracting new clients and assignments to its roster. As we have seen, it is inevitable that clients will be lost and will have to be replaced. Consequently, each agency has some kind of program designed to attract new advertisers. Sometimes one or more individuals are given that assignment as a sole responsibility. In other cases the job falls to top agency management. And in still others it is distributed among selected officers of the agency in addition to their other duties.

In addition to the above, some larger agencies offer an assortment of other specialized services which may include the following.

Marketing. A number of the larger agencies have marketing departments which complement or supplement similar departments on the client side. These departments perform studies and analyses of the marketplace in an effort to unearth additional sales opportunities for their clients' products or services. These opportunities frequently take either of two forms. First, identification of markets, or groups of consumers, to which a product can be promoted successfully by means of appeals especially designed for that purpose. Second, identification of untapped consumer wants or needs that can be satisfied through the introduction of some new product or service. Of the two, the latter is the more common search.

Publicity and public relations. For the most part, agency PR departments plan, organize, and execute programs designed to procure publicity for the client's products or services. Sometimes the PR objective is to build sympathetic understanding of the client's business problems or needs. Only a limited number of agencies have publicity or PR departments.

Sales promotion. Sometimes called merchandising, this is the task of developing point-of-purchase displays, promotional novelties, and a whole laundry list of items and devices designed either to draw attention to a product in its retail environment or to stimulate the performance of the client's sales force or that of other personnel whose activities can affect sales.

Direct mail. A small number of agencies have separate departments (or people) specializing in the planning and preparation of direct mail materials of one kind or another. Broadly speaking, however, most major advertisers perform this function for themselves.

TV program production. A very small number of agencies—whose clients prefer to sponsor tailor-made specials or spectaculars—have on their staffs one or two specialists whose job is to develop and produce such shows. This function used to be more commonplace in agencies when radio was the chief broadcast entertainment meduim, and although the practice continued for a while in the early days of television, it has now almost disappeared as a result of the networks' and independent production houses' having properly assumed this role.

Internally, each of these groups is likely to be structured differently from agency to agency. This matter will be treated in more detail in describing the workings and responsibilities of the various specialized assignments.

ACCOUNT EXECUTIVE
VIII SERVICE AND MANAGEMENT

This is a complex and wide-ranging function and one that calls for a high level of general advertising proficiency and sound business judgment. It is frequently identified as being the job of interpreting the client's needs to the agency and the agency's ideas and solutions to the client. Which is true, as far as it goes. But it grossly understates the full responsibilities of the assignment which include all the following:

Planning. In almost all agencies, no matter what their size, the account executive people are responsible for drawing up the advertising plan—the job that advertising is supposed to do, the idea that is to be communicated, the audience to be reached, the media to be used and the frequency of that use, the money to be appropriated for the purpose, and the measurement of the campaign's effectiveness (to whatever extent such measurement may be possible).

In order to do this job properly the account executive must be intimately familiar with all phases of the client's sales and marketing activities, including the sales and profit goals that have been set by the client. He must also have a sound understanding of what the client's competitors are doing in the marketplace, whether and why they are succeeding, the nature of their advertising activities, and roughly what they are spending and how they are spending it. He must understand and be familiar with all the trade practices that affect the client's marketing, the channels of distribution available to him, competitive pricing and promotional efforts, and any other influences that may affect consumers' buying habits.

In short, he must be an expert in his client's field of marketing.

Finally, it is essential that he know what advertising can and cannot be expected to accomplish. This may seem like an odd or obvious qualification. But it is a fact that advertising is called upon not infrequently to solve problems it cannot possibly solve. A plan that recognizes this fact and confines itself to assignments that are appropriate for advertising is generally off to a good start. One that does not can never succeed.

<u>Coordination</u>. It is evident that the plan requires the thinking and contributions of all kinds of specialists in the agency —the rest of the "account team." It is the sole responsibility of the account people to orchestrate these efforts and to see to it that all the components of the plan are brought together in harmony and on time. In order to accomplish this result the account executive must ride herd on researchers, creative people, media specialists, producers, and often outside suppliers. If it occurs to you that the person who has this job needs a variety of talents, he does indeed. Here is a catalog.

He must be familiar with a variety of research sources and have a working knowledge of their applications. He must know, above all, what research can discover and what it cannot, and he must have the judgement to initiate its use when it can be helpful and to avoid it when it cannot. When research is indicated, he should have intelligent opinions about what kind of research is indicated and the depth and extent of it that is needed.

He must be a good judge of copy and broadcast commercials, and he must ensure that the advertising addresses itself precisely to the task assigned to it, and does not wander off the point. He should also have an appreciation of art and commercial forms and techniques to help him appraise the material that he is going to present to his client. He must, in fact, be an imaginative and discerning critic. In this capacity, when necessary he should be capable of persuading his colleagues to the correct point of view without ruffling too many feathers. He needs judgment and tact, as well as the respect of the rest of the team.

He must understand the assets and liabilities of the various forms of media and be able to relate them to the problem at hand. He will not be asked to make detailed technical analyses of media types and individual media, but he should have well-informed and supportable reasons why magazines are best for one advertising assignment and television for another, for example.

He must be up-to-date on production requirements for both print and broadcast media, and the time and cost involved in the various methods available.

Last, but far from least, he must know, understand, and be able to motivate the members of his team, and the more he knows about the difficulties and complexities of their jobs the more effective he can be in that respect.

(In those cases in which his client makes use of point-of-sale material, contests, sales incentives, and other promotional devices he must also be well-informed about the latest sources, developments, availabilities and costs in these fields.)

Presentation. The account man or woman is always charged with the responsibility of presenting the agency's ideas and material to the client and of obtaining approval to execute the plan, or to prepare further advertisements, or to extend certain media commitments, or whatever other course of action may be indicated. Much of this is done on a day-to-day informal basis, of course. However, when the time comes for a full-scale presentation of a new plan, or a campaign that involves a departure from what is currently being done, the procedure usually becomes much more formal. There are two reasons for this. First, the agency will want and need to present the investigation, research, analysis and reasoning that led to the development of its new proposals—to set the background against which the new advertising is to be judged. Second, there will almost always be an unusually large audience from the client's organization. In addition to the advertising manager or director whom the account executive sees often, there will probably be people from marketing and sales management. Moreover, there will likely be representation from the research department, and in some cases the top management of the client's business—not infrequently including the chief executive officer.

Under these circumstances it is up to the account people to decide on the physical form that the presentation should take—on charts, on film, on slides, or an informal conversational type presentation; whether the advertising will be shown in rough layouts and storyboards, in semifinished form, or with type-set and illustrations and taped commercials; whether the recommendations will be set forth in great detail, or simply highlighted; and how many agency people will participate, who they are to be, and the role each is to play. It is a job not unlike that of the producer and director of a theatrical production.

Regulatory matters. As noted earlier, there is a growing number of regulatory agencies and a fast-developing body of precedent having to do with what can and cannot be said in advertising. The effective account executive finds it increasingly necessary to be familiar with this body of rules and laws and quasi-laws. He need not be a lawyer, but he needs to be well enough informed to know when to obtain qualified legal opinion in cases about which he has reasonable questions.

In addition to a knowledge of governmental regulations he should also be familiar with the various codes and practices of publishers and networks, and be prepared to negotiate with them on matters affecting the interests of his clients. To make things even more complicated for him, each of the three major television networks has somewhat different criteria relating to advertising acceptability.

Profit management. While the account supervisor or executive is keeping an eye on all the foregoing activities he must concern himself with the profitability of the account for which he is responsible. His management will be sure to remind him that if the agency does not operate at a profit it will not operate at all, and that his account is supposed to contribute to that profit. As a consequence, he must monitor the amount of manpower and time that his account uses up, and keep both to a minimum consistent with high quality agency service and performance needs. In the event that service requirements make profitability impossible, he must be prepared to work out with his client some kind of supplementary compensation arrangement, usually in the form of a fee.

In the smallest agencies there may be one or two account executives reporting directly to the head of the agency. In larger organizations there will be one or more account supervisors who report to the top man and who supervise the activities of a number of account executives. In the largest agencies another layer of management enters the picture in the person of the management supervisor—a person who is responsible for one very large account, or a group of accounts. There is a very rough rule of thumb which suggests that one man can keep his finger on the pulse of only between $12,000,000 and $15,000,000 of annual billings, and it is at this level of volume that the management supervisor usually is needed.

A word about the organizational structure of major advertisers is appropriate here. Most of them have highly developed tables of organization which call for several echelons of authority and responsibility, ascending from the assistant advertising manager (or product manager) to the vice president in charge of marketing. Typically, when an agency serves a client of this kind, an account person is paired off with each level of client activity—a junior account executive vis-a-vis the assistant advertising manager, the agency management supervisor with the client vice president in charge of marketing, and so on.

Where this is the case—and to some extent in less highly structured situations—the management supervisor or the account supervisor falls heir to another function not mentioned above. He gets into the personnel business. He must recruit, evaluate, hire, fire, promote, and otherwise manage the account people who report to him. More than that, and key to his success, he must assign the right agency person to the right advertiser counterpart. In doing so he must base his decisions as much on the personalities of the people involved as on their professional talents and attainments. In the agency world if you cannot get along with the client, you are pretty sure to have to get along without him.

IX   CREATIVE SERVICES

Here is the engine room of an advertising agency.

There is no legitimate function of an agency that is not important, as can be seen from the preceding chapter, but the end product of the agency is the advertising itself. That is what the public sees and responds to or turns away from. That is what the client is most interested in. That is largely the basis for the reputation and success of the agency. That is the payoff for all concerned.

The key figures in this activity are writers, designers and art directors, and specialists in supervising and managing the production of radio and television commercials—commercial producers. Not too many years ago it was common to find each of these specialities organized into separate departments, designated as Copy, Art, and Commercial Production. Now, however, the more widely accepted practice is to group all these talents together into a single Creative Department. This evolution sheds a ray of meaningful light on the nature of the agency business.

The departmental form of organization was oriented to the best interests of the management of the agencies, especially their profit performance, because a pool of writers (all considered versatile enough to work on any account the agency serves) offers valuable flexibility in the use of manpower. When the load on account X is heavy, get help from someone assigned to account A which is not too busy, and thus spread the work and keep everybody occupied and the number of employees to a minimum. The theory rests, as you can see, on the assumption that each member of the group is as well qualified to develop advertising for each client as every other member, but in practice—even though there are many versatile creative people who can perform as utility infielders—this assumption simply does not hold up. The reason is twofold. First, most advertisers have a tendency to demand that the people assigned to their accounts be knowledgeable specialists in their fields, and agencies are prone to accede to this kind of pressure. Second, the departmental setup has a profound psychological effect on the people involved because, for some reason, the lines around the boxes on the organizational charts seem to turn into real barriers to cooperation and teamwork—a sort of "you stay on your side, and I'll stay on mine" syndrome goes into action. Obviously such a state of affairs does nothing for the excellence of the creative output.

The best solution seems to have been to create self-contained groups of writers and visualizers, assign them to a specific client, or product, or problem and let them go to it. In this way they can stimulate and challenge each other and somehow produce ideas, and concepts, and advertisements superior to those they are capable of individually, or separated by departmentalization. It may cost the agency more, but it is worth it.

So now we have the writer, the art director, and the commercial producer working together, and any one of them can be the author of the bright new idea, the great new campaign, the concept that motivates the reader or viewer to go out and try the product or to give sympathetic understanding to the point of view expressed by the advertiser. Each member of such a group must have well-developed conceptual skills. This is to say he must be a first-rate advertising professional as well as a topflight technician in his own specialty. And one of the strong points of the group operation is that good people working together tend to nourish and develop each other's abilities almost unconsciously. On-the-job training the painless way.

After making allowances for the blurring of responsibilities caused by group organization and action, there are still specific capabilities that each specialist must have.

The writer first. To begin with he must be able to write to the audience that he is addressing, and above all his writing must be clear and persuasive. It can be formal, technical, or colloquial—whatever the assignment calls for—but it must register the idea that the underlying advertising plan prescribes. When promoting products, the best writers create advertisements that contain one simple idea expressed with clarity, memorability, force, conviction, and persuasion. When engaged in the communication of more complex ideas, they set forth clearly, logically, and convincingly the arguments in support of the premise that the advertiser wishes to establish. Only a handful of writers are equally good at both tasks. Most are at home with one, more than with the other.

The writer must have also a highly developed appreciation of design and illustration as they contribute to the communicative value of the printed word; should be sensitive to the fact that illustration (or illustrative technique) is often the most compelling element in an advertisement; and be facile enough to accommodate his writing to the visual aspects of the presentation of an idea. Similarly, he must understand and be sympathetic to the nuances of commercial production techniques and be able to see in his mind's eye how they can advance the cause of the product, service, or proposition that the advertising espouses.

The writer must have a thorough understanding of the uses and lessons of research—copy research in particular—so that he can take advantage of those techniques that are known to be successful in attracting the reader's or viewer's favorable attention. There is considerable body of well-documented data dealing with effective handling of both the visual elements and verbal construction of advertments. These data provide valuable guidance for the designer, the writer, and the commercial producer alike. The wonder is that they are so often ignored—to the detriment of the finished product. In any case, help is at hand for those who take the trouble to become familiar with these resources, and who are willing to use them.

The writer—like the account executive—must be acutely conscious of and up to date on the legalities that bear on the claims that can be made for the product or service which he is attempting to persuade people to buy. He will be well-advised to insist that test results or other representations provided by his client are an absolutely reliable and unequivocal basis for his advertising assertions. For, if they are not, both his agency and his client face embarrassment at best, and remedial action ranging from a publicly delivered rap on the knuckles to damaging litigation, at worst. Although the writer shares this responsibility with others, he will wisely assume that he is solely responsible in accordance with the precept of prudence. To wit: "When something is everybody's business, assume it is yours alone and be safe. Assume it is someone else's and be sorry."

Writers do not live in ivory towers carefully sequestered from the world around them and completely dependent on the information and direction they get from their account management counterparts. They need the enthusiasm and the intellectual curiosity that will lead them to go out into the marketplace and see what is going on—to find out what the customers are doing and thinking, and what the trade (storekeepers, clerks, salesmen, distributors, and agents) are up to and what their concerns are. In short, the best writers have a very clear and current idea of the environment in which their advertising is appearing, and if they are professional they will buy and use competitive products for the sake of comparison and education. (Admittedly, writers cannot be buying new cars, pianos or expensive stereo equipment every week; but demonstrations, observation and listening can serve much the same purpose.)

Writers need also to mingle with their clients, to get to know them, to become acquainted with their ideas and points of view. In many instances the writer will be called upon to present his copy or commercials himself. When he does so he must be able to put forth the thought processes that went into the development of the advertising and to make a strong and convincing case for what he has created. In these situations he becomes a salesman to some degree, and if he turns out to be a good one his career will benefit accordingly.

Taking this assignment one step further we come to a job that is found in most agencies having technical or "industrial" accounts. It is called "copy-contact," and it combines the writer's craft with the account executive's function, as one individual does both jobs. In the majority of cases a copy-contact person writes for and serves an advertiser whose customers are readily identifiable and are known to be readers of highly specialized publications edited to appeal to their interests. Over-simplified, the assignment for the advertising here is to extol the virtues of a manufacturer's equipment as a fulfillment of the readers' needs—a given brand of earth-moving machinery for the highway construction industry, for example.

In the big agencies creative departments are thickly populated and require management and supervisory activities. In such operations there are usually groups of creative people each headed by a group supervisor—who directs the activities of his people, assigns projects to them, monitors their activities and edits and polishes their output. In turn, these group supervisors report to the supreme creative being whose title likely is Vice President of Creative Services, or Creative Director. He is one of the key members of the organization and therefore one of its top officers. As such he must be concerned with the caliber of people on his staff and with many of the other personnel responsibilities that go with such a job.

Here again we encounter one of the very thorny problems of agency management: to find a man for the top creative spot whose creative credentials will command the respect and admiration of his department's members and who is a good administrator at the same time. There aren't too many of them around. In fact, many a brilliant creative person has been promoted to this assignment only to be a miserable failure as a manager and to be frustrated by the wide differences between administration and making advertisements. Blessed be the agency which employs the person who can fulfill both roles with distinction!

The visualizer. "Visualizer" seems like a contrived word, and it is. But it is useful for our purposes because there are so many terms that are used to describe the people who design the printed advertisements and conceive and direct the video part of television commercials. For instance, they are called layout men (or women), designers, art directors, and sometimes simply artists. By whatever name, however, they create the illustrative material that makes the advertising come alive and capture the attention of the reader or viewer. In fact, in many instances it is the picture or sequence of pictures that constitutes the message—often with hardly any copy at all.

These people tend to have special skills and talents, just as writers do. Some are best at designing for the printed page; others excel at creating commercials. An acceptable analogy is that some artists favor oils, some pastels, some watercolors, some gouache, some pen and ink, and so on.

Looking at the print side of the business first, it becomes apparent that the visualizer must have great competence in design. He must be able to arrange the various elements of type and illustration so they are harmonious, clear, uncluttered, arresting to the eye of the reader, easy to read, and capable of conveying the advertising message quickly and accurately. It is important that he have a good grasp of the variety of type faces and sizes that are available, and he needs an appreciation of the niceties of spacing and margins as they contribute to the readability of his layout. This may sound slightly precious or inconsequential, but every one of us—trained in design or not—can assay the significance of these details simply by examining a group of advertisements chosen at random. Some are pleasing and easy to read, but an unfortunately large percentage are not. Parenthetically, this disparity of quality grows out of one of the continuing challenges of the agency business; namely, the thrust for innovation and novelty (so essential to success) against the counterforce of time-tested techniques and principles. The balance is not always easy to find.

The visualizer also needs a sense of what illustrative technique will contribute most to the ultimate effectiveness of the advertisement. Should the finished artwork be an artist's rendering (and, if so, in what medium) or should it be photography (and, if so, what kind of photograph—muted and/or suggestive, or brilliant and sharply detailed)? These considerations may seem minor, but they can have a profound effect on the quality of the finished product and, therefore, are of real consequence.

Once the visualizer has determined the art form best suited to his purpose, he must take the next step and help to decide which artist or photographer is best qualified to produce the effect or mood that he wants. This decision is sometimes complicated by the constraints of the budget.

It goes without saying that these several specialists almost always have a background of training in an art school or a school of design, and can draw or sketch with enough facility to be able to prepare rough layouts for their clients' approval prior to ordering the finished artwork. They are, however, not normally called upon to do the finished illustrations to be reproduced in the publications in which the advertising appears.

It may be that the attributes and requirements of a competent print visualizer can be framed in more precise terms than those of a first-rate commercial producer. Certainly the range of alternatives available to the former is not nearly as great as that at hand for the latter, who can summon up all the almost magical processes, devices, and techniques of film and tape recording. The commercial producer has many strings to his bow, including animation, superimposition, close-ups, long shots, studio effects, location scenery and backgrounds, fade-outs and dissolves, and a host of other optical manipulations. To be truly professional he needs to have a working familiarity with them all. Moreover, he must know which one is most likely to reinforce the persuasiveness of the message—again, with an eye on the budget established to get the job done.

Commercial production is an art form in evolution, and one that demands great sensitivity and understanding on the part of those who direct it. The best producers may have a preconceived idea of the desired effect when they start to shoot a commercial, or they may frankly experiment on the set until they develop something that satisfies them both commercially and artistically. This is the "I'll know it when I see it" school and it is not at all uncommon. But, in whatever fashion it comes about, the effect is the thing.

All this is not to say that the field of commercial production is an uncharted wilderness, because there are obviously many techniques and approaches that have been subjected to research of the most painstaking kind. A couple of examples serve to make the point. It is known, for instance, that humorous animation works well for certain product categories, but carries no clout at all for headache remedies. It is also a fact that one of the most successful advertisers in the country has achieved many outstanding marketing successes by relying on consistent use of "slice of life" commercials—to the horror and dismay of most intellectual critics. So there are some reliable roadmaps even at this developmental stage of the art, and the producer must study them and use them, although he need not follow them slavishly.

It was acknowledged earlier that commercial production is much like producing and directing a Hollywood movie. It is. But in case this particular field of activity seems too exotic and difficult for the beginner to contemplate it will be heartening to know that there are many highly skilled and extremely competent independent commercial production houses in all the major cities, and that these resources can be relied on heavily to lend their experience and expertise to agency people whenever they are needed.

There is also a sub-specialty of commercial production in the larger agencies. It is the job of the casting director, whose assignment it is to screen applicants for parts in commercials and to select those most suited to whatever requirements have been established. The casting director must keep a file on the available talent and must know all the talent agencies and the kind of actors they have on tap. He must be proficient enough in the field of television to evaluate the appearance, mannerisms, and voices of actors in context with the mood and purpose of each commercial to be produced. And he must spend many hours in auditioning and screening job applicants.

X   TRAFFIC CONTROL AND PRINT PRODUCTION

These activities are combined in some agencies, and kept separate in others. But no matter how they are accommodated they work together very closely, and it is not always easy to tell where one leaves off and the other begins. Nevertheless, we will try to sort them out for the purposes of this book.

Traffic control is the tower at an airport, or the switch tower at a railroad freight yard. It is where the status boards are kept and where timetables and deadlines govern everything that goes on. It has the responsibility for seeing that all the components of any kind of advertisement are fitted together and forwarded to the designated medium in the proper form and *on time*. The material can range from the type and illustrative elements needed for engravings or photoreproduction of print advertisements, or to the electrical transcriptions of radio commercials.

The people who work in this department of an agency usually do so under considerable pressure for two main reasons. The first is that time is always short and (as seen through the eyes of the traffic people) everyone else involved drags his heels in the development of every advertisement, and that includes the client. The second is Murphy's Law: "If anything can go wrong, it will." But because of that pressure, or in spite of it, there is real satisfaction to be had from every successfully completed assignment.

A good traffic planner needs above all to be orderly and well-organized—to be able to array and manage large amounts of detail, and to do so with accuracy. He must be totally knowledgeable about the various processes that are involved in the creation of an advertisement, with particular emphasis on the minimum amount of time needed to complete each step along the way. And he must be able to keep track of, and nurse along, a considerable number of simultaneous projects, all in different stages of development.

He must be able to deal effectively with outside suppliers and with the members of the creative team(s) with whom he works. He must know which creative people respond to persuasion and cajolery, and which have to be browbeaten in order to get them to attend to the details that most of them abhor but that his performance depends upon. He must, in brief, be a moderately successful jackknife practicing psychologist. And to maintain his equilibrium he must enjoy his trade.

The job is a demanding one, but for those who do it well there is great solace in the incontrovertible fact that this function supplies the indispensable lubrication for the agency's gears.

In some agencies traffic control reports to top creative management on the theory that it is an integral part of the complete creative process. In others it reports to some other boss—often the agency's business manager—on the theory that it is mighty hard to excercise meaningful control over the man who can deny you a pay raise or fire you.

Print production involves some of the record-keeping and all the sensitivity to timing that are present in traffic control.

The production person is charged with buying the various elements that go into the makeup of every kind of printed material produced by the agency. This means not only advertisements, but booklets, pamphlets, brochures, outdoor posters, car cards, flyers, presentations, sales manuals, and direct mail letters and other similar material. The volume and variety of the agency's output will depend on the kinds of accounts that it has and the assignments that it either solicits or is given.

TRAFFIC CONTROL AND PRINT MANAGEMENT

Production people deal with a great number of outside suppliers who provide a very substantial bag of services. Chief among these are typographers, engravers, electrotypers, photo-reproducers, photostaters, printers and, in some cases, free-lance artists, Accordingly, it is necessary for production people to have a catalog of all the available sources for each of these services and to know the strengths and weaknesses of each supplier.

It is important to note that budget control is a high priority item on the producer's list of responsibilities. Thus, he or she needs to know to whom to turn to get a job done and the price tag that is likely to come along with it. In many instances, too, competitive bidding will be standard operating procedure on some accounts—which usually means securing bids from three different suppliers, and always means extra delay and record keeping.

Like the traffic controller, a good production person needs to be well-organized and capable of close attention to detail, while processing a number of projects simultaneously. It is not an assignment for someone who is easily distracted or who is prone to panic. Also, like the traffic controller, the producer must be absolutely certain of the time that is needed for each of his suppliers to complete their assignments under normal circumstances, and the irreducible minimum that they need under the most severe pressure that he can bring to bear.

Here again is a little glimpse into one of the recurring and frequently sticky agency problems; namely, how does one keep the cost within the budget and at the same time get the work done with the blinding speed that is often called for? If you have the solution you can write your own ticket in any agency you choose.

Both traffic control and print production can be career jobs for those who find them sufficiently rewarding, but for the most part they are stepping stones to other and better paid jobs in an agency—generally in account management. It used to be that every beginner in an agency started in the mailroom or in one of these functions as a trainee. The practice is far less common now, but it is still essential that both account people and creative people fully understand what these activities are all about and how important they are to the smooth operation of the whole machine.

Art buying. As mentioned earlier, there is still another function that is closely related to both print production and visualization. It is the job of buying the artwork with which to illustrate the finished advertisement. In some agencies the supervisory people in the visualization operation do it. In others, it is done by specialists who work hand in glove with the visualizers. Sometimes these specialists report to the head of the creative activity, and sometimes they are incorporated into the production assignment. But whatever the structure, the job is one that requires knowledge, taste, bargaining ability, and close liaison with the creative people who have contrived the advertisement and whose baby is thus being born.

There are many parallels here to the responsibilities of the casting director. The art buyer must have an extensive portfolio of information about the talents and particular skills of a large number of commercial artists whose media range from photography to oil painting. He must know, for instance, which photographer is best qualified to do mood shots of children for certain kinds of advertisements, and which is most proficient at taking dramatic pictures of heavy machinery—and everything in between.

As many artists are capricious, one of the key pieces of information that the art buyer must have concerns the reliability of all those in his stable of suppliers when it comes to meeting firm delivery dates. The ideal artist for the job may be the least dependable, and when time is of the essence, prudence often dictates giving someone else the call. Another insight that the buyer needs relates to the temperament of the available artists, since some of them are highly cooperative with the creative people and are willing to try their best to create the impression that is sought, and others are inclined to substitute their own inter-pretations—sometimes causing friction and delay.

The art buyer is governed by the same budget con-siderations as are the other phases of print production and must be able to negotiate prices that are acceptable to the client. Sometimes this is done by securing formal bids, but usually it comes down to the buyer's familiarity with the price scales of the people he deals with. So the buyer must exercise a certain amount of good business judgment in the conduct of his work.

Art buying is a fascinating occupation for anyone who has a true appreciation of the whole spectrum of commercial art forms; who enjoys dealing with interesting and talented people; who gets satisfaction from discovering and helping to make a success of newcomers on the scene; and who is sufficiently well organized to maintain the kinds of records needed to make the whole process run smoothly and professionally. It is a rewarding career for those whose inclinations and aptitudes fit them for the role.

XI   MEDIA SERVICES

There is an old saying that "any advertising that runs is good advertising." But it is not true. Good advertising must be seen or heard by the right audience to be effective. And that is where media services come in, for the media department of an agency has the responsibility for selecting and recommending the publications or networks or stations which are to carry the advertising. And next to the advertising itself, nothing commands as much of an advertiser's attention as do media questions, because reaching the right people is critical to the advertiser's success. Money spent for advertising which reaches the wrong people is money wasted.

There are three major functions that every agency media department must carry out in order to perform properly. They are research, selection, and buying. These functions take place regardless of the internal organizations of such departments, most of which are fairly much alike.

Since Chapter V contains a reasonably complete dossier of the available forms of media and the general uses to which they are put, it would serve no useful purpose to rehash them here. Therefore, let us go on to a broad description of how a media department works and the kinds of opportunities that it offers.

Media research is where the process begins. Every agency has at least a basic media research library. The larger ones subscribe to many different research services. Together, they supply an almost overwhelming amount of data on reading and viewing habits, and profiles of the readers and viewers attracted to various publications and programs. One of the primary sources of this information for the media person is a set of publications called *Standard Rate and Data Service.* These books list newspapers, magazines, radio and television stations and the costs of differing units of space or time that they offer for sale—including any structure of discounts that the advertiser may earn if he uses a certain number of pages or spots, instead of only one. Also listed are the paid circulations of each of the publications, and the number of families in the area covered by each radio or TV station. For many years the selector had only this service as his basic tool. It told him how many copies of a magazine were bought each week or month, but nothing about the people who bought them. It told him how much six advertisements cost in periodical X and how much in periodical Z. He could divide the circulation figures into the advertising costs and find out how the cost of reaching a thousand buyers (not necessarily readers) compared in the two magazines. Beyond that, however, he had to rely on his own assessment of the editorial content of each publication and the material furnished him by the publishers in order to form an idea of the make-up of the readership.

The media selector had even less precise information about broadcasting stations. He knew their wattage, their cost, and he had a very rough idea of the area covered by their signals. To this he could add his own evaluation of the kind of people likely to be attracted by each station's programming—if indeed there was anything to distinguish one from another.

So it's not hard to see why additional measuring services came into being. Everybody involved got a little fed up with wondering whether their overseas steamship advertising was being directed to people who always went to their cottage at the lake, or if their dress pattern advertisements were being skipped over by readers who bought their clothes from Sophie or Givenchy. Inevitably when more intelligence became available it came in a rush from many different suppliers, who used varying techniques to obtain the information and, consequently, drew differing pictures of each medium's readers or listeners. So now, of course, the media expert has a different kind of problem. He must decide whose service he will believe.

Despite problems arising from the lack of compatibility of his information sources, today's media researcher—and the selector whom he or she supports—is light years ahead of his counterpart of 20 years ago. He has an acceptable understanding of the demographic configuration of the audiences of all the major magazines and network programs.

Moreover, he is well on his way to a better fix on what is called psychographics, or the measurement of the attitudes and life styles of readers and viewers. It is possible for him to identify those media choices that reach the greatest number of heavy users of certain product categories, as opposed to those whose audiences use relatively little. It goes without saying that these are important breakthroughs, because now an automobile manufacturer, for example, can be reasonably certain that his advertising is being directed to new-car buyers rather than used-car buyers. Similarly a miller can single out those media that have a good following of home bakers. And so it is in one category after another.

In addition to these refinements we also have the wonders of computerization to help the researcher sort out the data and apply it to the project at hand. Roughly, it works this way: an advertiser has a large budget and the advertising plan calls for the use of both network TV and magazines to reach women between the ages of 24 and 35. The aim is to achieve the maximum possible reach (gross numbers of such women) with the greatest possible frequency (average number of times an accumulated audience is exposed to the same advertising message within a measured period),within the established budget. The media selector arrays a list of magazines and programs which are likely candidates for the assignment, and turns the list over to the researcher. The researcher, in turn, asks the computer to provide that combination of media that will get the desired result with the greatest efficiency. The computer provides the answer, complete with all the necessary mathematical documentation. And there you have it, except in those instances in which time on one of the desired programs is not available, and then the whole process has to be repeated.

The media researcher keeps voluminous files of other pertinent, but less esoteric, information about both publications and broadcasting stations. For example, almost all the so-called "trade" publications can and do supply data with respect to their readers—the companies they work for, their titles, their responsibilities, and their responses to the editorial content of these magazines. Similarly, broadcasting stations make available their own data concerning the characteristics of their audiences and the degree to which they respond to station promotion and other broadcast material. All this knowledge is of great value to the person whose task it is to decide where to propose that the client spend his money.

From the foregoing it may appear that the media researcher is merely a dispenser of information who caddies for the selector. To some extent that is true, but it is the least important of his duties. Where he really earns his keep is in evaluating and collating the data and information that are available. He must understand thoroughly the techniques used in developing such data and be able to pass judgment on their reliability. His is the voice that says the agency will or will not subscribe to such-and-such a service, and why it will or it won't. He must be professional and proficient in all aspects of his chosen field. Moreover, he must be imaginative and creative enough to interpret the data he deals with, as well as being able to identify other areas of exploration that will supply even more grist for the selector's mill. He needs the keen, analytical mind which finds statistical investigation absorbing and fascinating.

Media selection is the task of using the available information to put together, in the most precise fashion possible, the combination of media that will be seen or heard by those people most likely to respond to what the advertising has to offer.

As noted, it starts with an understanding of the audience(s) to be reached, the action or reaction that is hoped for, the creative platform—spelling out whether color is needed, whether the message is to be long or short, whether there is a creative requirement for television or the printed word, whether the force of frequent repetition is wanted—and the money available in the budget. In short, adherence to the basic advertising plan.

The first step is to identify one or more categories of media that fit the bill in a general way. From that point on the selector engages in a process of refinement, cut and fit, until he and his research support—with computer contributions—arrive at the most promising recommendation attainable. This may sound like a routine job of juggling figures around until the puzzle is completed, and in some cases it is. On the other hand, there are all kinds of opportunities for the selector to exercise imagination and arrive at truly creative solutions to his problems. Since numbers are not everything, the mood, or tone, or atmosphere of a given medium can be of great significance in the selection process and deserve thoughtful consideration and evaluation.

After all, someone had to be the first to imagine the "Bell Telephone Hour," or the "Hallmark Hall of Fame," or to recognize the unusual audience delivered by telecasts of tournament golf, or to work out rotogravure inserts in daily papers, or to negotiate cover fold-outs in nationally circulated magazines. The list is a long one and stands witness to the value of creative initiative in this field of agency work, as in all the others.

In addition to his in-house bank of data and information the selector is continuously exposed to a succession of sales pitches and presentations from representatives of the various media. In order to keep himself informed and up-to-date he must spend a very considerable amount of time listening to these representatives, discussing his views with them, and assessing the validity and value of what they tell him. Some of this time is spent in the offices of the agency, and some at formal luncheon presentations or informally over a lunch table. In fact it is a standard agency joke that free lunches are a part of a media selector's pay. If that is so, there are those who believe it is hard earned money.

As an aside, it is the writer's opinion that the best of all media presentations are those that provide real insight into the intangibles of the medium—things like the purposes and policies of the enterprise under discussion, its aims and ambitions, the responsiveness of its audience, and the influence that it has been able to bring to bear in its field. So long as the selector has all the statistics back at the office anyway, his perception and proficiency will be advanced best by his understanding of these vital but hard-to-measure insights. And the deeper and broader his knowledge of all the attributes of all the programs and publications, the more professional and constructive his recommendations will be and the quicker his rise to the top of his profession.

To be a good selector a person should be analytical, at home with figures, imaginative, interested in the broadcasting and publishing businesses, and well-informed about them. He or she should take pride in doing an efficient and scientific job, and should want to develop a feel for the nuances and intangibles of the various media that make the difference between routine selection and really great work.

Media buying is largely an extension of the selection function and comes into focus most sharply in contracting for radio and television time, and particularly spot buying. What happens here is this: the buyer is given the specifications against which to seek the best spots for the advertiser's purpose. He or she then finds out from the stations, or their representatives, what spots are available. (These are called "avails.") Armed with this information he then negotiates for the purchase of those "avails" that will best meet his specifications and budget.

Here "negotiate" is the precise word, because the rate structures of most TV and radio stations and networks are flexible, to say the least, and a knowledgeable buyer can extend his client's budget appreciably by skillful negotiating.

Buying space in publications and on outdoor boards is much more routine. Rates are fairly stable and the problem of availability is almost non-existent. Negotiation with these media consequently revolves around the position that the advertiser wants in a publication—back page of a magazine, sports page of a newspaper, and so on—or the specific locations of poster boards.

As mentioned earlier, the initial phase of spot buying is done by oral agreement—as is some of the print buying. It is essential to the success of both buyer and seller, therefore, that they live up to their oral commitments in later written confirmations. Integrity is of the essence.

A good buyer must be a good trader, a facile handler of detail, a good analyst of the data used to measure the "avails," and a good worker under pressure. When a buyer gets busy, he gets very, very busy, even by agency standards.

Buying often is a stepping-stone to selection, supervision, and more lofty management jobs, although there are some people who enjoy it enough to make a career of it.

XII   MARKETING

For the most part, only the larger agencies have marketing departments—and not all of them. Nevertheless, almost every agency engages in some form of marketing research, even though it may not always be very sophisticated.

Consequently, we again need a definition of terms in order to understand what we are talking about.

Marketing has been described, written about, and redescribed *ad nauseam* in recent years—sometimes with a singular lack of clarity. The process, or function, can be defined quite simply, however, as planning and organizing to make a product that people want, at a price they are willing to pay, in the form that they like, and to distribute it through the kinds of retail outlets where they would expect to find it. Basic marketing is the kid on the corner with the lemonade stand. Go into business when the weather is hot; set up the stand where the traffic is heaviest; add more sugar, if the customers like it sweeter; and adjust the price to what the traffic will bear.

Marketing research is the kind of investigation that helps the manufacturer understand the opportunities available to him and the various pricing, packaging, promotional, and distributional constraints which the marketplace can be expected to impose on whatever venture he may consider undertaking.

There was a time when manufacturers figured out what they could make profitably and then tried to sell it—regardless of whether it filled a consumer want or need, as judged by the consumer. That approach has been found wanting and is seldom followed today. Instead, most manufacturers of consumer products now have their own marketing staffs to guide them in the development of new products that will appeal to the person who carries the marketing bag. Many such manufacturers feel that they are fully competent to carry out this function without outside help, and as a result, the agencies that work for such clients find that they do not need special marketing staffs.

On the other hand, there are a number of very successful marketers who believe that an outside point of view—the perspective and objectivity of an independent organization—is a useful adjunct to their own internal operations, and call on their agencies to supplement their in-house work. Sometimes, too, these marketers turn to marketing consultancy firms for such outside counsel. In any event, the activities of the advertiser, the agency, and the consultant tend to parallel each other in this field. They all do the same kinds of things, and all are staffed by the same kinds of people.

What sorts of things do marketing departments do? The list is a long one. All that will be attempted here is the enumeration of the more important and more common tasks.

New products. On the theory that standing still is equal to falling behind, most modern manufacturers are constantly on the lookout for opportunities to develop new products that will add to their lines and, hopefully, to their profits. It is up to the marketing people to spearhead this search, using all the research tools and accumulated wisdom they can summon to the job. In the simplest terms, this requires that they know what products are out there; how well they are doing; what gaps they are leaving, if any; and what kinds of new entries might fill those gaps *at a profit.*

Generally speaking, they seek new product openings for merchandise that is compatible with the producer's manufacturing and distributional facilities. It should be acknowledged that those who favor the conglomerate philosophy of corporate expansion do not concern themselves too much with this consideration, and it is probably too early to pass judgment on whether they are wise or foolish.

Product refinement. It is an increasingly evident phenomenon that, in many categories of consumer goods, products tend to dry up after a relatively short life. They seem to lose their appeal in their conventional form. When signs appear that this kind of weakening is beginning to take place the makers start looking for ways to do something that will give their aging items a shot of adrenalin. This may take the form of a new formulation, a new ingredient, a new package, a new selling appeal to a different consumer segment of the market. And in some cases, new channels of distribution are adopted. Everybody is familiar with the "new and improved" basis of persuasion. And to paraphrase General Forrest, the name of the game here is "to git thar fustest with the newest."

New audiences/new uses. Often, marketers feel that there may be ways to expand sales and profits beyond those available from the traditional users of a product or service. So modern marketing people are constantly seeking ways to make their products attractive to broader and different groups of consumers, or to devise new purposes for which such products can be useful. An outstanding example is "TEFLON*" which was originally conceived as a special purpose commercial lubricant, but which became a huge household success when it was applied to cookware as a non-stick coating.

Competitive studies. It has been recorded that marketing experts need to be completely informed about competitive activities, successes, and failures in the marketplace. Easier said than done. In practice an impressive amount of time and effort is devoted to such intelligence gathering and analysis, and the operative question is always "why did it happen?" It is no great feat to observe that product A is an enormous success whereas product B has laid a king-sized egg. The trick is to develop a clear understanding of the multiple variables that contributed to the

*TEFLON is Du Pont's registered trademark for its non-stick finishes.

health of the winner and the illness of the loser, and to profit by what has been learned.

Research of various forms is critical to such analyses, and will be summarized a little later.

Merchandising. This is a loosely used word with many meanings. The dictionary definition is very similar to that of "marketing:" "The promotion of sales by presenting the right product to the proper market at the right time, by carrying out organized advertising, using attractive displays, etc." Currently, however, "merchandising" is generally used synonomously with "sales promotion." It relates to promotional activities at the retail point of sale. Included are such things as special packaging, posters, display devices, incentives for retailers and salesmen's contests, give-aways, cents-off deals, coupons, sampling, tie-ins with related products, and on and on.

This is a highly specialized activity that usually is undertaken by the advertiser, working with his outside suppliers. Sometimes, however, it is carried out by his agency. In either case, it is most effective when it is closely coordinated with the advertising. Maybe the most familiar example of full-scale, all out advertising-merchandising efforts are those mounted by the Gillette Company in connection with such events as the World Series.

Recently many marketers and marketing people have begun intensive studies of trends in consumer habits, attitudes, and buying practices in order to be able to anticipate opportunities for new products, or new uses or markets for existing ones. This is a sensible and forward-looking thing to do, because as habits and appetites change, competition changes too. Whereas the auto maker may have once thought his only major competition for the sale of a second car was his competitors' latest models, he's now aware that it may be a boat, or a swimming pool in the back yard. It makes a difference.

Trend reading is not yet an exact science, however, and one of the better "trenders" is the first to admit that it is not easy to spot the difference between a trend and a fad—certainly not at first. And in a business that prefers the word "challenge" to the word "problem," this is a real one.

Whatever planning, studying, analyzing, or evaluating the marketing man or woman is engaged in, he must always keep one thing in the front of his mind: his recommendations must reflect his best judgment of how the consumer—the person who lays out the cash for the product or service—will act, react, or perceive the offer, whatever it may be. This means that if the laboratory cannot formulate the product as prescribed, forget it. If the factory cannot produce the product as prescribed, go no further. If the optimum price cannot be made to be profitable, scrub the whole idea. If the proper channels of distribution cannot be set up, no go. It would not be inaccurate to suggest that more new product launchings have foundered as a result of injudicious compromises on one or more of these points than for any other reasons.

One of the oldest cliches is still sound: if the dogs don't like the dogfood, they won't eat it.

Marketing research is the basis for all marketing decisions. It need be neither sophisticated nor esoteric, although it often is. But it should provide enough pertinent and usable information on which to predicate sensible and rational decisions. It may be helpful to put down some of the kinds of fact finding that properly come under the heading of marketing research. In spite of the fact that they vary in complexity and technique, they all are used in any first-class marketing activity.

Government statistics. There is an almost unbelievable amount of information to be had from the Bureau of the Census, the Department of Commerce, the Department of Labor, and other subdivisions of the Federal government—as well as from state and municipal sources. As we might suspect, there is more information on file somewhere in Washington or in the state capitals than anybody will ever know what to do with. Bureaucracy demands the collection of statistical data, even though, like bales and bales of I.C.C. material, it may be stored unopened in some remote warehouse along the Anacostia river

In any event, it is there to be mined and a great deal of it is readily available and extremely useful. Probably the single most useful and manageable summary is a fascinating book titled the *Statistical Abstract of the United States* which reads a little like the *Guinness Book of World Records*, but can be used for practical commercial purposes.

Business statistics. Various trade associations and other organized business groups compile facts and statistics about one field of activity or another (the petroleum industry, the automotive industry, the dairy industry, etc.) and these go into great detail about the ramifications of each such trade or industry.

Client information. Every client organization served by an agency marketing department has on file a substantial amount of detailed information about its own business and about that of its competitors. This resource is the point at which most marketing analyses start. In essence it tells the researcher the limits of present knowledge, and is likely to suggest what additional information is needed in order to arrive at a final understanding of the problem or opportunity.

Syndicated services. There are a few highly regarded sources from which the manufacturer can learn about the movement of his, and his competitors' goods at retail. These services are vital to the makers of packaged goods sold in supermarkets and drug stores as well as other mass merchandise outlets. They tell them what people are really buying, instead of leaving them at the mercy of what their salesmen or the retail store managers think or estimate.

The manufacturer can obviously measure the flow of product out of the factory door. But without services such as these he has no reliable way of knowing whether that flow is building up excess inventory at retail, or whether it is moving through into the hands of the consumer. Thus, these "audits" are of great value to anyone who wants a true picture of the marketplace.

Calling on the trade. In spite of the above rather negative remarks about the reliability of salesmens' reports, it is important for researchers to "get out into the field" and see what is happening at the point of sale. This is particularly true when the product in question is sold through franchised outlets (like automobile dealerships), or where the performance of the retail salesman is a key factor in the movement of goods, as in the case of major appliances sold through department stores. By being there when it happens one can see if the client's product is being compared unfavorably with competitors' products by the retailers, or whether a particular model is being used as a loss leader in order to entice buyers to come in to be traded up to a more expensive model—with a higher dollar mark-up for the dealer.

Such retail activities are far from uncommon, and a first-hand exposure to them makes the interpretation of statistical data much more enlightened and perceptive.

Specially commissioned research. Frequently the motivations and attitudes of various consumer groups are hazy and, therefore, only a matter of conjecture to the advertiser or to the agency. In such cases it is customary to employ specialized independent research services in an attempt to measure such opinions and attitudes. However, as large-scale studies of this kind are both costly and time-consuming they are generally approached with caution. Unfortunately, when the price of the research becomes a problem, action is often taken on the basis of someone's "assumption." When that happens the "assumption" had better be right, because the cost of operating on the basis of a faulty "assumption" can be many, many times the cost of the needed research.

Parenthetically, this kind of opinion research presents the practitioner with two challenging and absorbing problems: first, being sure that the study is properly structured to get accurately reliable results; and second, being able to interpret it intelligently and to delve beyond the superficial findings. Much has been written on this subject, but suffice it to say that sometimes the answers that are not adduced are more significant than those that are.

Pilot research. This is a short form of the more penetrating opinion studies just mentioned, and is very tricky stuff indeed. Here it is decided to interview a few people in order to "get a reading on what they think." A straw in the wind, as it were. It is quick and inexpensive, but when it has been done it is likely to lull people into thinking that they have a definitive study they can rely on absolutely, and if they do the results can be disastrous.

One senior research executive describes this phenomenon as "the tyranny of numbers." It is his contention that once someone records on paper the fact that 80% of the respondents say this or that, the 80% becomes gospel, even though what it really means is that 8 out of 10 people who were chosen because they were handy—as opposed to 40,000 out of 50,000—indicated a point of view.

The truly valuable function of pilot research is to find out whether a given set of questions can be answered sensibly and intelligently by a broader cross-section of the population. It is fine to use it that way. But to rely on it as substantially meaningful is to play marketing Russian roulette.

Consumer use panels. Testing consumer reaction on the basis of actual use is a common method of obtaining a presumably objective appraisal of new or modified products. These tests are sometimes done to find out simply if the product performs, or behaves, or tastes as the marketer hopes that it will; and sometimes as a comparison to other popular products. In this latter case, it is usual to disguise the identity of all the products used.

Unfortunately, there are dangers in this procedure as well. The principal one is that the product being tested often is carefully hand fashioned and tests well, whereas the production line cannot match the test batch, and the consequent loss of quality shows up unfavorably in the real marketplace.

Group interviews and discussion panels. These gatherings are employed to generate ideas for new products, new uses for existing products, and natural every-day expressions and descriptions that can be used in advertising and promoting merchandise. Usually, they are devices for guiding the preparation of advertising copy.

What characteristics must the top-flight marketing man or woman have?

To begin with, he or she must be imaginative (there's that word again), practical, and profit-oriented. It should be clear from the foregoing that this is not a job for dreamers and academic theorists. The marketing specialist is dealing with real people, real competition, and real dollars. And if he is working in an agency, those dollars belong to the client who usually looks upon them with understandable affection. In fact, he is likely to find himself another agency if they are treated disrespectfully by the incumbent.

He must be knowledgeable about the marketplace, and he ought to work like a beaver to keep up with everything that is going on in it. If he is to be good at his trade, his curiosity will assure that he enjoys such work. If he does not find it enjoyable, he should seek employment elsewhere.

He must be an avid follower of trends and developments in consumer attitudes, opinions, habits and life styles—not only in connection with the specific product or service under his charge, but in all others as well. The reason is that there are frequent opportunities to adapt an idea or practice from one category of merchandise to another. This procedure is currently called "lateral reasoning," which is a splendid euphemism for borrowing someone else's ideas—sometimes identified as plagiarism.

Like others in the agency, he should be a perceptive amateur psychologist with considerable sensitivity to what makes people tick, and why they behave as they do.

The good marketing man or woman should be a star at evaluating the marketing implications of the research findings available to him, and should be competent to initiate courses of action based on such readings.

He should be a clear and persuasive communicator with better than average writing skills, because he will frequently find himself espousing courses of action that have not been traditional in his client's business. In such circumstances he will need to present his recommendations in a carefully reasoned and coherent fashion, aware that "it is human nature to resent criticism and to resist new ideas."

Finally, he or she needs plenty of "chutzpah." Remember that the agency marketing specialist is often in the position of advocating that the client undertake innovative programs that may involve large sums of money. When he does so he must be able to face up to his client, look him in the eye, and say with confidence: "If I were in your position, I would be willing to risk the stockholders' money on this undertaking." The faint-hearted need not apply.

What about the market researcher?

The cliche is that this person should be "good with numbers." That may be true, as far as it goes, but it is a woefully inadequate characterization of the needed attributes, particularly in an age when electronic calculation tends to obsolete the human mathematical machine.

The marketing researcher, first and foremost, needs to know how to structure research programs and procedures. He needs to know what kind of research to employ, and to be able to see that it is applied in an unbiased and responsive manner. He needs to be able to analyze research results in a way that uncovers any possible bugs in the technique used to collect the information and makes allowances for any irregularities that may show up.

Like the marketing specialist, he must be good at analysis and interpretation as well. He must, in short, be a professional in his field—because that is what he gets paid for, not simply for his aptitude for manipulating great quantities of figures.

An ability to report findings clearly and concisely is also a requisite for success, because he will be dealing with somewhat impatient businessmen who are going to want responsive, comprehensible answers to questions like, "What does it tell us?" . . . "What does it say?." And inasmuch as those businessmen have paid for the research, they are entitled to unambiguous answers.

Finally, he should share with the marketing specialist an almost overwhelming desire to know "How come?."

A reminder. This chapter has assumed that the reader may be exploring functions and job opportunities in the advertising agency business, but marketing and marketing research activities (and the qualifications for working at them) are essentially the same, whether in an agency or in the client organization which the agency serves.

XIII PR, PUBLICITY AND SUPPORTING ACTIVITIES

Some agencies have a number of specialized departments one of which is known as the "Public Relations Department," which is usually a misnomer.

Public relations is just what it sounds like; the art of relating the affairs of an organization to the public interest, and of communicating the actions of a company to the public. It was best described many years ago as being "95% what you do, and 5% what you say." The net result of adherence to this doctrine is that true public relations counselors, or consultants, advise their clients more with respect to their actions than to their words. In doing so, they deal with the very top people in the company they serve.

This is not a customary function for any advertising agency. On the other hand, as noted above, agencies that have PR departments engage extensively in obtaining publicity for their clients' products or services as well as for individuals in the client organizations. Therefore, it would be more realistic to call these "Publicity Departments," although that would not sound as impressive.

How does publicity differ from advertising? Largely in the fact that advertising is paid for and is worded and placed exactly as the advertiser wishes. Publicity is not paid for and is worded as the carrying medium chooses. The medium has no authority to alter or edit an advertisement, but it can treat a publicity release in any way it sees fit. It can use as much or as little as it wishes, headline it as it wants, use it when convenient to the medium rather than the publicist, and add its own interpretation (favorable or unfavorable) to the release. Moreover, the extent to which any publicity material may be used depends on the medium's assessment of its news value, or its inherent interest to the readers or viewers to whom it will be exposed.

It is apparent that publicity not only lacks the timeliness and control that characterizes advertising, but that there are some risks in the way that a medium may treat publicity material. On the other hand, it does provide exposure for the product or service in question. And of transcendental importance, skillfully prepared publicity material appearing as editorial matter, implies independent and valuable third-party endorsement on the part of the medium in which it appears.

Publicity can take many forms and has many uses, and what follows may be considered but a sampling of the most common activities in the field:

New products or services. In fields in which there is a genuine public interest, there are many examples of straightforward news and picture releases that are accepted almost verbatim by the various media. Familiar instances include the introduction of a new airplane, or inauguration of a new passenger ship service, or the arrival of a new category of automobile. These are hard news, and placements are easy to make. The true challenge comes in getting coverage for items of characteristically low public interest value.

Product demonstrations. Many household and personal use products lend themselves to demonstration on TV talk shows of one kind or another, and some (like the semi-miraculous self-developing camera film) find their way onto the nationally telecast evening news programs.

Case histories. Some product categories lend themselves to the development of histories of use that are of interest to specialized audiences. This form of publicity is closely akin to advertising, and case histories developed for publicity purposes often are also converted into advertisements.

Newsworthy promotional devices. Some categories of merchandise have enough intrinsic interest to the public to make it fairly easy to construct events that will capitalize on that interest and thereby become bona fide news. The annual fashion shows of the latest creations by name designers, and the annual diamond ball are familiar instances.

Use of prominent personalities. Occasionally items of rather limited interest can be publicized by the endorsement of public figures whose activities and views are news in themselves—and who, incidentally, are not averse to picking up a little spending money in this way.

Contrived events. The list of such goings-on is a long one, but a couple of examples would be "Bat and Ball Night" at baseball parks, and the all-time stroke of genius that resulted in the appearance of Mr. Gaedel, a midget, as a pinch hitter in a major league game in St. Louis.

Day-to-day activities. There are many routine publicity activities which are necessary, but not very glamorous. They include such things as announcements of the election or promotion of a company's officers; the opening of new (or sadly, the closing of old) plants; the appointment of an executive to the chairmanship of some community enterprise; and other similar developments.

Personal publicity. This kind of activity is designed to increase the fame and stature of business executives. It usually involves ghost-writing their speeches and learned articles, and arranging for them to appear as panelists on talk shows or at business gatherings of their peers.

(With respect to much of the above, it should be acknowledged that the line between certain types of publicity and merchandising, or sales promotion, is often very fine indeed.)

THIS IS ADVERTISING

Financial publicity or PR. This is a highly specialized sub-division of the trade which deals with earnings reports and related subjects, including preparation of a company's annual report to its stockholders. It sounds quite simple and direct, but the catch is to report in such a way as to influence the financial community favorably, while not being incendiary in the eyes of labor unions and Federal regulatory bodies.

PR advertising. Advertising is frequently used as a means of telling the public about a company's problems, policies, activities, and goals. In time of war, or during periods of shortages or other unusually trying circumstances the volume of this kind of advertising always increases very sharply. It is usually referred to as PR or corporate advertising.

Accomplished practioners of professional public relations need to have mature judgment and a complete understanding of all their client's management problems—especially labor union and governmental relationships. Moreover, they should possess also an almost unerring feel for public attitudes as they affect the client. And equally important, they should have the strong support and confidence of the client's top management.

First-class publicity people need a highly developed promotional flair, advanced writing skills, keen perception of what is and is not newsworthy, and as many useful connections with the various media as they possibly can develop. Finally, in some specialized fields they require a depth of technical knowledge as well.

Other Supporting Activities

So far this discussion has dealt with jobs and functions that are more or less unique to advertising agencies and the advertising departments of their clients—the kinds of things that first come to mind when people talk about "being in advertising." There are, however, a number of other things that must be done in an agency, as in any other business, and their performance may differ slightly from their counterparts in other commercial endeavors. A brief listing of them follows.

Financial management. This particular function deserves more than passing mention, because it is awfully easy for an agency to go broke if its financial resources are not managed with great care. The reason can be stated with the utmost simplicity. Almost every agency, large or small, will be obligated to pay the media and the suppliers with which it does business from two to two-and-a-half times its *total net worth each month*. We have seen that the general practice is for the agency to be paid by its clients before it pays these obligations, and so long as that happens everything is smooth sailing. But sometimes things go wrong. There are delays. And when they occur the agency may become bankrupt, at worst, and lose its reputation for financial responsibility, at best. Consequently, the daily cash flow of an agency should be a matter of prime concern to its management.

Most of the larger agencies have both a treasurer and a controller to monitor their cash positions and to ensure prompt collection of bills, as well as prompt payment of supplier invoices. There is no hard and fast rule for the assignment of duties to these people, but typically they break down this way:

The treasurer is responsible for investments (long and short term), insurance, leases, stock transactions, and the regular monthly treasurer's reports.

The controller is responsible for seeing that the agency's bills go out on time and are paid on time, and for the payment of bills to outside firms. He also oversees the agency's accounting procedures, arranges for annual audits of its books, and keeps track of the cost of serving each client's account.

These people are backed up by the necessary clerical, secretarial, and supervisory personnel—whose qualifications are the same as those for similar jobs in other businesses.

THIS IS ADVERTISING

In-house legal counsel. Earlier, the point was made that advertising law and administrative regulations are still in the process of development and refinement. The result is that most larger agencies now have one or more lawyers on their staffs as advisors to creative and account management people, and also to deal with whatever outside legal counsel the agency may employ.

This is a highly specialized form of law, but like anything else in a formative state it can be both intriguing and challenging.

Office management. This is one of those vital, but relatively thankless, chores that must be attended to daily. It involves all the necessary housekeeping functions of any business. It may include personnel management, and sometimes supervision of the agency's computer operation, if it has one. (In other forms of organization the computer people usually report to either the treasurer or the controller).

As agency people are highly individualistic, the office manager can be sure that he or she will never have enough corner (or outside) offices to go around, and that whatever furniture may be on hand will not suit a high percentage of the agency's employees.

Basic support. To keep them running, agencies (like every other business) rely on secretaries and typists, receptionists, librarians and information specialists and clerical people. If the agency has a computer facility, it will also need keypunchers, programmers, analysts and machine operators.

There is nothing special about these jobs in any agency, except that they take place in a lively environment, among interesting people—altogether a stimulating atmosphere in which to work.

Administrative assistants. Many agencies follow the practice of using administrative assistants in office management, account management, personnel, print production, media, and research. Jobs of this kind serve a dual purpose: they reduce the operating costs of the agency, and they provide valuable training for beginners.

PR, PUBLICITY AND SUPPORTING ACTIVITIES

These jobs deserve consideration by young men and women hoping to get started in the business.

XIV

ADVERTISER AND MEDIA FUNCTIONS

So far the burden of this discussion has been on jobs and functions in advertising agencies. There are, however, opportunities in advertiser operations and in media employment, and as the advertising department of an advertiser company is reasonably analogous to an agency, let us start with that.

There are many companies which advertise but do not employ agencies. In such organizations the advertising department does all the things that an agency does. It performs the same functions and is likely to be structured pretty much in the same fashion.

When such a department is identified as an operating unit of the company to which it belongs many media organizations will not grant it the customary 15% agency discount. The theory is that they are dealing direct, and not through an agent, and therefore there is no justification for the agent's discount. This posture has obviously led to many heated disputes. For the most part, however, many media organizations hold the line. If this situation causes you to wonder about the economic basis for such a company policy, be assured that it has puzzled others as well and that the companies' financial benefits are moot.

One way out of this dilemma has been to set up so-called "house agencies" which have the appearance of being independent but actually are wholly owned and controlled by the advertiser company they serve. In such circumstances the discounts are taken by the house agency and the financial picture makes sense. As of this writing there has been endless discussion of real or imagined operating advantages and disadvantages of such arrangements. At every large meeting of the Association of National Advertisers papers are read and speeches are made concerning the house agency. The belief here is that into the foreseeable future those who advocate house agencies will adhere to their position, and those who disagree will not change their views. The idea of setting up a house agency will continue to have some economic appeal. It all seems very simple. The profit the agency normally makes accrues to the coffers of the advertising company.

Some who have set up their own house agencies have found it seems to work for them. Others have been disappointed to discover that the quality of the creative product, or the absence of certain specialized services, or the failure to make the hoped for profit gave them second thoughts about the whole idea.

In any event, the discussion has taken on almost metaphysical overtones and cannot be resolved here.

The more common arrangement is for a company to have an advertising department that works with an agency, so let us take a look at what that does, how it works, and how it is staffed.

First of all, it is the unit with which the agency has almost all its dealings. It sets the advertising policy for its company, establishes the advertising goals, ensures that the advertising is consistent with the company's sales and marketing objectives, and transmits management thinking and decisions to the agency. If it is a good department, it is the principal source of all the pertinent information the agency needs—either directly or by providing access to responsible executives in other corporate functions.

It is held accountable for the performance of the agency —for the efficacy and quality of the advertising plan and the advertising the agency produces and places. In that capacity it usually has the power to approve or reject the agency's recommendations. In this connection it should be noted that it always has the power to say "No" to the agency. In some cases, however, final approval of the agency's work can be granted only at a higher level of management.

In some organizations it has the authority to hire and fire agencies. In others it has only the authority to recommend such action, with the final decision again at a higher level. As a rule of thumb, the more important advertising is to the sale of a company's products, the more top management makes or influences the final advertising decisions.

In corporations which have more than one agency on their strings the advertising department is responsible for directing and coordinating the work of the different agencies—particularly with respect to purchases of media. This involves preparing and keeping master schedules to ensure that all volume discounts are earned. Another responsibility is to make sure that no one issue of a magazine is scheduled to carry too many advertisements for the company's various products while the next issue may be scheduled to carry none. In some cases this responsibility is delegated to one of its several agencies, which then becomes known as the "agency of record." As such it places all, or most, of the company's advertising, including that produced by other agencies.

The advertising department is in charge of the advertising budget which includes expenditures for time and space, production, materials, and all the internal costs of the department.

Some advertising departments also create and produce direct mail material, or promotional and point-of-sale pieces. (In some instances, as we have seen, this work is done by agencies.) Regardless of where these activities take place, it is the function of the advertising department to keep promotion and advertising coordinated, directed toward the same goals, and similar in focus and tone.

THIS IS ADVERTISING

In smaller companies the department is headed by an advertising manager who may have only one or two assistants. In multiple product corporations the department is likely to be headed by an advertising vice president, or a director of advertising, who presides over the activities of separate advertising groups, each under the direction of an advertising manager. In the first instance, the advertising manager usually reports to the sales manager. In the bigger operations the advertising director generally reports to the marketing manager or vice president, and may be on the same organizational level as the sales manager. In some corporations the advertising department is a staff function, assigned to advise and support line activities like sales and marketing. In others, it is a line function in one of those departments. There is no general rule.

Sometimes the department has its own research unit, and sometimes there is a separate research department that it calls on for whatever help it may need.

In the case of the smaller companies the agency account executive usually deals directly with the advertising manager, one on one, and if they both know their business, communication is clear and simple. Moreover, decisions are fairly readily reached and well understood and things proceed in an expeditious fashion. In the case of the larger companies, matters tend to get more complicated, because it is usual for each level of authority in the advertising department to be matched by a comparable level in the agency. The advertising director transacts his business with the agency's management supervisor; the advertising managers, with account managers; and assistant advertising managers, with assistant account executives; ad infinitum.

This practice is fine in theory and looks very orderly on an organizational chart. But it has a tendency to become unglued when the human element enters the picture. Take a hypothetical case involving only two levels of decision making. The agency account executive presents a commercial to the advertising manager, who likes it but is afraid that his boss will not. He suggests some modification, or a change in direction, and the account executive goes back to the agency and reports what has happened. The commercial is redone and again presented to the advertising manager, who approves it. Now the account supervisor presents it to the advertising director (who knows nothing of this history). He does not like it. His subordinate has guessed wrong about what will appeal to him, and then the commercial goes back to the drawing board once more. When this takes place much time, expense, and mutual confidence is squandered. And when there are as many as four layers to work through the opportunities for this kind of backing and filling and second-guessing in advance are greatly compounded.

These pitfalls are, of course, widely recognized in the business, but as yet no one has been able to devise a fail-safe way to avoid them.

Be that as it may, advertising departments are staffed very much as agencies are—the same kinds of people, often doing essentially the same kinds of jobs. The critical difference is in the power to make the final decision and to commit the advertiser's money.

Finally, the advertising director or manager needs many of the same skills and abilities as the account manager or account executive, and the other specialists—whether writers, artists, researchers, or media people—must have the same qualifications as their agency counterparts.

Media advertising departments

The advertising departments of all forms of media have a dual role. On the one hand, they function just as the advertising department of any other business that advertises. On the other hand, they are the space or time selling arms of their publications, networks, or stations.

With respect to the first function, there is little to add to the description of any other advertising department, except for one difference in emphasis. It is this. Media rely much more heavily on promotional and publicity devices and activities than do firms which sell consumer products of some kind. They also are relatively heavier users of direct mail than most other advertisers, and for a very good reason. Much of their effort is directed to persuading other advertisers to use their facilities, with the consequence that their audiences are easy to define and to isolate. In situations of this kind direct mail is tailor-made for their purposes. The result is that their advertising staffs are largely populated with creative people whose talents run strongly in this direction.

The other assignment of these media advertising departments is to sell space or time. Accordingly, they employ a sales force that calls on advertisers and their agencies in an effort to persuade them to use the medium they represent in preference to competitive media.

The selling that they do is of two kinds: individual, person-to-person persuasion, and presentations to groups of agency and advertiser people. This latter activity usually involves the use of sophisticated graphic and projection techniques and promotional material.

These departments are managed by an advertising sales manager or advertising sales director, depending on the size and scope of the organization. The head man, whatever he is called, is most likely to be a particularly effective personal salesman. He may or may not have strong administrative credentials or pronounced creative promotional facility.

In addition to the creative people and the sales people, there is usually a strong research group in these departments. Research is important because much media selling is based on the "numbers game"—how many total readers or viewers, their demographics, their psychographics, the cost of reaching a thousand of them, comparisons with similar numbers trotted out by competitors, and so on. The researchers in these departments need the same qualifications as those in agencies, except that the focus of their assignment is on the use of their statistical material as a selling tool rather than as a basis for dispassionate appraisal. It is not characteristic of media to publish research findings that reflect on them unfavorably. They are more likely to leave that task to their competition.

There is little to add about the skills and attributes required of creative and research people in media advertising departments as they parallel those of similar agency specialists. However, it may be appropriate to comment briefly on the qualities that make a good media salesman. He, or she, should be personable, articulate, persuasive, and extremely knowledgeable about his medium and its competitors—*particularly as they relate to the needs and objectives of the prospect he is soliciting.* This means that, like an agency account person, a really good media salesman should spend a lot of time and considerable effort studying and understanding the prospect's business, its problems and opportunities, and the competitive pressures that bear on it. There is nothing worse than a media representative who approaches an advertiser, or his agency, with a solution to a problem that does not exist. But the phenomenon is not unheard of.

XV EDUCATIONAL PREPARATION

It can be seen readily that different educational backgrounds will be appropriate for the different specialties in advertising—both in agencies and in other organizations. The key word here is *specialties*. The person who is interested in becoming a designer, for instance, obviously needs to be instructed in that field. It is, however, not nearly as clear that an aspiring account executive should specialize in any particular curriculum.

In fact, there is probably more disagreement with respect to the best preparation for advertising than with any other facet of the business. To some extent this may arise from the educational experiences of those interested in the question (built-in bias). To a degree it may result also from observation of the diverse backgrounds of the more successful practitioners—and they are indeed diverse. (See details on last page of this chapter.) Whatever the reason, there is no unanimity of opinion and as a consequence what follows represents one man's view, shared by some others, but not endorsed by all.

It may be helpful to try to sort out some of the major considerations that confront the beginner and to comment briefly on them.

Is a college degree necessary? Necessary, no. Highly desirable, absolutely! As in almost any form of endeavor there are some outstanding examples of extremely successful advertising men and women who did not go to college, or did not complete the normal four years. But these are relatively rare, and they have done it the hard way. So it is unlikely that many of them would advocate attempting to go directly from high school into an agency, unless the individual intended to go to night school to make up for what he or she had missed. Also the hard way.

There are some fragmentary statistics on this subject which tend to show that the percentage of agency employees having college educations runs in the high eighties. So if you are not already in college that should be your next step.

Should one major in advertising? At the risk of being thrown out of the lodge, my answer is "no." Such early specialization tends to screen out too many other courses and experiences that will be of great value later on. As we have seen, agency work confronts the people in it with an unusually broad range of problems and situations in a variety of businesses and industries. It therefore makes sense to prepare for an advertising career by being equipped with an understanding and appreciation of as many fields of endeavor as possible. Where curiosity and initiative are at a premium it follows that a grounding in a manageable number of disciplines is sure to be both valuable and supportive. Put another way, in advertising today it is virtually impossible to know enough about enough. And while college is the place to start it is not the place to begin to compartmentalize one's knowledge.

On the other hand, if the decision is made to adopt advertising as a major, there is a limited number of colleges which offer full courses in the subject.

If not advertising, then what should one's major be? Here again there are several schools of thought. Some say economics, some psychology, some English; and each opinion has some basic validity—economics for an understanding of the marketplace; psychology for an understanding of what motivates people and how they react; and English to sharpen skills in writing and communication generally. Quite obviously all are worthwhile, and a fundamental knowledge of each of them is to be desired, along with some appreciation of other subjects included in the category of liberal arts.

In some institutions it is now possible to elect more than one subject in which to major. This makes the decision somewhat less difficult. But where you are forced to choose one specific field as your major, the vote here would be cast for English, and not simply for the time-honored reason having to do with facility of expression and command of the language, although it is a perfectly valid one. A much more persuasive argument for concentrating on and becoming steeped in English literature is the insights it provides into history, social outlook and attitudes, and the evolution and recognition of the legitimate rights and appetites of all the people—with emphasis on their philosophy, psychology and behavior.

Neither space nor the patience of the reader will permit detailed development of this thesis here, but the proposition can be verified by an analysis of the reading matter in any four-year curriculum of English literature—the chronological sequence of the authors, the subjects that commanded their interest, and the periods of which they wrote, from pre-Shakespeare to post-Steinbeck.

What about postgraduate study—a master's degree? Once more the experts tend to think differently. Some believe that an MBA is important because marketing is what the whole thing is all about, with the creative aspects of advertising being only a part. Others theorize that such a degree may be of significant value to someone who is headed for a career in marketing management, but that it may represent educational overkill for most advertising agency jobs. They contend that much of its instruction can be readily absorbed on the job by anyone who puts his mind to it.

A fair posture may be one which says: A postgraduate degree is unquestionably valuable—particularly so for those intending to go into account work or marketing—but that it is not essential to a successful advertising career. This would seem to be borne out by current estimates which show that roughly 10% of the people in the larger agencies hold such degrees. It is probable that this percentage is much smaller in smaller agencies.

In the final analysis the matter boils down to a realistic assessment of your own personal situation and inclinations. Tough-minded answers are needed to questions like: Can I afford it? Can I ask my family, or my wife, or husband to help underwrite it? Have I a bona fide thirst for additional academic instruction, or am I merely putting off the evil day when I have to go to work? Am I eager to get started on a job? Am I willing to study on my own time in addition to holding down a full-time job?

These, and other questions like them, can be answered only by each individual in the light of his or her own circumstances, and they must be addressed soberly and thoughtfully. No matter how the answer comes out, the person who undertakes this exercise seriously will have had a useful experience in reasoned decision making.

What about extra-curricular activities? The more they can be worked in and the closer they relate to advertising, the better. Those that come to mind first, of course, are such things as working on school and college newspapers and magazines, and at broadcasting stations. Any kind of involvement with these ventures is good, and it need not be confined to the advertising side of the operations. Announcing, reporting, and editorial chores all will help to familiarize you with the practicalities and problems of the communications media, the environment in which advertising appears.

During vacations it helps to advance the cause if you can find some kind of a summer job with one of the media, or with a printing house or a film studio, even though the assignment may be lowly and the pay very modest.

Another useful part-time task is work as an interviewer for some research organization and, since this avenue of approach is not quite as obvious as some others, the chances of being taken on should be fairly good. A tour of duty of this kind will not only demonstrate the trials and tribulations of getting respondents to answer questions, but will provide a chance to study the structure and technique of the questionnaires as they affect people's willingness and ability to respond to them.

Many counselors also advise part-time employment in any form of retail selling that results in contact with purchaser behavior at the point-of-sale. Work at the check-out counter of a supermarket, or in a department store or at a service station will provide valuable experience in observing the real world of merchandising in action—both from the point of view of the seller and of the buyer—and will supplement theory and book learning in a practical way. It also helps on one's resume, about which more will be said later.

Finally, many of us find it difficult to the point of incoherence to stand up in front of a group of people and address them. As advertiser jobs, and agency jobs, and media jobs demand a lot of this kind of activity it is a good idea to prepare for it. This can be done by taking courses in public speaking, or by engaging in community theatricals, or through debating societies, or in any other manner that helps to develop "presence" and puts you at ease on your feet facing an audience.

All the foregoing requires participation in some organized routine, and there is nothing wrong with that. On the other hand, there is a solitary method to prepare for an advertising career that can be undertaken in your own way, at your own convenience, at your own pace, wherever and whenever you want. It is quite simple, and consists of asking yourself questions about the advertising that you are exposed to every day. Questions like: who is the advertising supposed to appeal to? What are they supposed to do about it? Is there one central idea or message that comes out of it? Is it trying to sell the whole category of goods (often the case when one product has the lion's share of the market), or is it selling the specific product's competitive merits as compared with other entries in the same category? Does it seem to be based on some kind of basic research, or is it obviously trying to capitalize on a trend or a fad? Does it seem to be realistic, or is it farfetched? Is it contrived, or natural?

Maybe it can all be summed up in one basic query: why did they do it that way? The idea may sound difficult or complicated as set forth here, but it is not. In fact, it can be both stimulating and entertaining, and may lead to attempts to improve on the output of the professionals, which would be a significant first step into an advertising career. It is well worth a try.

NOTE: On Educational and Occupational backgrounds:

The intention was to present some acceptably organized stratification of such backgrounds in order to substantiate the validity of the assertion. It has proved to be impossible to do so because a random sampling of the credentials of some of the more important officers of just one major agency turned up the following assortment:

- former trainees having degrees in academic disciplines ranging from architecture to psychology.

- one ordained protestant minister.

- one professional soldier.

- one ex-professional golfer.

- one senior media executive who started as a promotion writer.

- several refugees from the legal profession.

- two or three former magazine editors, one now serving as an account supervisor.

- a substantial group of former newspaper and magazine writers who have moved on to other kinds of agency assignments.

- people with a bachelor's degree in advertising, communications or business administration.

- people with a master's degree in the same curricula.

- a former sales representative of an automobile manufacturer.

- one sales engineer.

- one ex-policeman.

- etc.

XVI   COMPENSATION

There seems to be a living legend that all advertising people are walking around like King Midas with a brief case. Do not believe it. Most beginners earn salaries that range from modest to reasonably good, and established professionals earn pay that Dun & Bradstreet would say averages in "the middle five figures." Only a few who founded their own agencies at a propitious time and under auspicious circumstances have made a great deal of money. But even these have not accumulated fortunes comparable to those amassed by very successful entrepreneurs in other lines of business.

At one time, in fact, the very best and biggest agencies started their trainees at ridiculously low pay on the theory that it was a privilege to receive training in their exalted surroundings. They felt it was gracious of them to pay anything at all. Fortunately the increasing number of reputable and successful agencies has changed all that. Starting salaries now are at a reasonable and competitive level and the key word is competitive, even though every beginner is firmly convinced that his counterpart at another agency (or with an advertiser company) is being paid more than he is.

The American Association of Advertising Agencies conducts periodic surveys of what its member agencies pay their employees at various levels of responsibility, by function, and distributes the findings to its members. The surveys show that salary scales are fairly comparable from agency to agency, with but two broad exceptions. The first is that there are some built-in adjustments for the cost of living in different parts of the country. And the second is that, except for the very top people, pay scales are now lower in the smaller agencies than in the larger ones.

There are two basic reasons why the average agency employee does not make "fabulous" sums of money. The first is that between two-thirds and three-quarters of the cost of running an agency is its payroll. Therefore, the lower the total payroll expense, the greater the profits for the owner or owners. The second is that agency income can be affected drastically, and frequently without warning, by its clients' decisions to cut their advertising appropriations, in which case a swollen payroll becomes financially unsupportable. Prudent agency management is acutely aware of these facts and behaves accordingly.

In the first instance, management tries to get along with as few people as possible, preferring to avoid the anguish of large scale dismissals in hard times. In the second situation it is customary to keep salaries at a sensible level and to supplement them by other arrangements to be discussed later.

An indirect consideration of agency management is the level of pay established within major client organizations. It can be embarrassing if, or when, an advertising manager finds that his agency counterpart is earning substantially more than he is. So the fact is that, job for job, advertiser and agency salaries tend to be reasonably comparable.

The story is different, however, with respect to media salesmen who are frequently paid in accordance with the amount of business they bring in. Some of them do very well indeed as a result of such arrangements.

By and large, it is a safe generalization that the countrywide demand for qualified young men and women has resulted in an increasingly consistent level of pay standards from one industry to another. And advertising is no exception.

Basic salary is one thing, but what about the other goodies—the fringe benefits? Here it is dangerous to make sweeping statements, because an examination of the policies and practices of different agencies discloses only one indisputable fact: no two are exactly alike. There are, however, some characteristics that are common to a majority of agencies, in spite of the fact that their specifics are likely to differ.

- More and more agencies now have profit sharing trusts, established to provide nest eggs for employees who stay with them for a number of years. Some of these are contributory, and some are not. But in either event an amount equivalent to a given percentage of each employee's salary is set aside and invested in a trust fund annually in the name of the employee. Whatever the amount, these moneys accrue to the employee and are paid at the time of retirement or other departure from the agency, according to the terms of the trust agreement.

- Fewer and fewer agencies have pension plans, largely because profit sharing plans are correctly deemed to result in greater rewards to the long-term employee.

- Group life insurance is a common benefit.

- Many agencies provide (pay the entire cost of) employee travel and accident insurance.

- Blue Cross and Blue Shield protection is afforded by practically all agencies. Sometimes paid for by the agency, sometimes by the employee, and sometimes shared by both.

- The same thing is true of major medical (catastrophe) coverage.

- A lesser number of agencies also provides long-term disability insurance, either wholly paid for by the agency or on a co-op basis.

- At the higher levels of management the great preponderance of the agencies has an executive bonus, or profit sharing, arrangement. The amount distributed depends on the profit performance of the agency for each fiscal year, and the management's assessment of each recipient's contribution to that result.

- Ownership of agency stock is another prerogative of increasing responsibility and contributory performance. There is a considerable variety of ways in which this is made possible, but the end result is to help key members of the group to build an estate that will afford them some security when it comes time to retire.

To sum up, there is a good living to be made in an agency —with earnings in the top 10% of the national spectrum—supported by reasonable to generous ancillary protection, and an opportunity to build up a meaningful competence for the future —plus an outside chance to strike it rich.

XVII   APPLYING FOR A JOB

It should be recognized that applying for a job can be, and often is, both a little frightening and frustrating. The aspirant comes to the experience eager, confident that he or she has the requisite qualifications, in a hurry to get started and, not infrequently, somewhat short of ready cash. Whoever is doing the hiring is wary, dubious about any newcomer's ability to perform, uncertain of the applicant's credentials, and in no hurry whatsoever. He has made mistakes before and does not wish to repeat them. If he is a decent person, he recognizes that hiring someone who is not fully capable of doing the job is always more of a hardship on the employee than on the employer. So he is inclined to be quite deliberate in making his decision. As a consequence job-hunting takes patience. It also takes thoughtful organization, involving at least the following steps:

Self-analysis, which sounds harder than it actually is. It merely requires you to sit down calmly and dispassionately and to assess your strengths and weaknesses. For example, do you get along well with people, and do you understand and sympathize with their problems and aspirations? Are you outgoing, or reserved? Are you analytical, or intuitive? Are you methodical, or have you a tendency to shoot from the hip? Do you work well under pressure, or does it tend to fluster you? Do you take kindly to details, or do they make you impatient? Have you any ingrained bias about where you want to work, or are you prepared to go anywhere and move about at the convenience of your employer? Have you attributes, skills, and a yen for any identifiable specialized assignment? What kind of useful (or applicable) experience can you bring to the job you are looking for? Have you had any military duty?

In short, the thing to do is to decide what you want to be and to do in advertising and then to make a catalog of your assets for such work, as you understand it. And if, in the process, you discover certain liabilities, resolve to correct them.

Market analysis. This simply means informing yourself about where the kind of a job you want is most likely to be found and planning to prospect that territory. If you want to work for a big agency, you head for the major advertising centers. If you want to work for a small agency as a starter, you might well check out the opportunities in the less populous cities. And the same applies for jobs with advertisers and media.

Resume preparation. Most people, at any stage of their careers, approach this task with some trepidation. The problem always is to say enough to arouse interest and convey assurance without overstating accomplishments and qualifications in a way that turns off the potential employer. The solution, however, is to be found in following some fairly basic rules:

1. Be as concise as possible.

2. List *relevant* employment and activities in reverse chronological order. (The most recent job first.)

3. Neither overstate nor understate achievements that reflect your capacity to perform. (If you are inclined to be modest, do not forget that the person looking at your resume can only make a judgment on the basis of what he is reading. And if you are inclined to be on the flamboyant side, remember that over-enthusiastic claims in support of your ability are sure to reduce the credibility of what you have said.)

4. Include academic achievement as well as work experience and extra-curricular accomplishments. In this

connection, be sure to include any evidences of leadership attributes (team captain, class officer, etc.); for this is a quality that is in great demand.

5. Record information about *pertinent* hobbies or leisure time activities: painting, photography, short story writing, music composition, for example. But not polo, or flagpole sitting.

6. State relevant personal facts like age, date of birth, marital status, number of children, etc.

7. Give references. These should be the names of three or four people whose judgment and opinions about you are likely to carry some weight. Be sure to ask their permission first, and remember that the more responsible they are, the more honest will be their assessment of you.

8. Prepare your resume on standard size 8½ x 11 inch paper, as many busy people are likely to get rid of awkward sized printed material quite promptly.

9. Do not forget to include your post office address and phone number.

It is also a good idea to write a letter to go with your resume registering the kind of job that you hope to get, and why you believe yourself to be qualified for it—but *not* what you hope to be paid to do it. Salary discussions come after you and your future employer have decided that there is a mutually acceptable opening for you.

Supporting evidence. If you have written essays, stories, or advertisements, keep them and put together an attractive and well arranged scrap book (with your name on it) so that your talents can be recognized. If you have had experience with one of the electronic media, have smartly packaged tapes with you to serve the same purpose.

Moreover, if you have letters of recommendation (or of commendation), assemble these and either attach them to your resume or make them part of your scrap book. Remember that the name of the game is to bring to bear as many endorsements of your "employability" as you possibly can.

Introductions. Under no circumstances be reluctant to ask friends, friends of your family, or former employers with whom you have a satisfactory relationship to provide you with introductions to people who might have a job for you. They will not regard such requests as an imposition. On the contrary, they will get pleasure from helping you to get started. As someone has wisely said, "The way to make a man a friend is to get him to do you a favor."

Interviews. It goes without saying that you should always be on time for an interviewing appointment, and that you will get good marks for good manners. First impressions are important.

Interviews are likely to be somewhat nerve wracking, because you will be expected to do most of the talking and the line between running off at the mouth and not saying enough is hard to define, particularly if the person you are talking to sits there stone-faced and mute. Consequently, you should organize what you are going to say beforehand, with emphasis on why you want a job with *his* company (not why you want *a* job; he knows that) and why you think you are qualified to get one.

You will want to come prepared with intelligent questions about the kind of work available and the kind of contribution that you can make. Then listen intently to his answers for clues to ways in which you think you can fit into the picture. Try to establish a dialogue instead of a monologue, and whatever you do, do *not* ask questions about such employee benefits as vacation policies, pension arrangements, medical and other insurance coverages, or anything else which suggests that you are more interested in what the company can do for you than in what you can do for the company.

Perseverance. Unhappily, very few job applicants are hired at the first place they visit; and the process of getting on someone's payroll is often tedious, time-consuming and discouraging. So at first do not let your hopes run too high, nor your early disappointments run too deep. Make up your mind that getting the right job—like most other worthwhile achievements—requires a systematic approach, hard work, determination and persistence.

Good luck!!